Judyth

MW01618240

Thank you for helping with Paint the State!

Lori Otter :)

Ida Tours the 44

A Book of Idaho's Counties

Ida Tours the 44: A Book of Idaho's Counties

ISBN 978-0-9788868-6-8

Ida Tours the 44

A Book of Idaho's Counties

Presented by Lori Otter
First Lady of Idaho
Office of the Governor

Boise State University with the generous support of the Walmart Foundation

The series focuses on Idaho and the West. From history to natural wonders to the diverse people found in the Gem State, topics in this series appeal to our youth from preschool through high school. Titles in the series are also designed to provide connections to a variety of K-12 curriculum content, making each publication a respected, fun Idaho resource for schools. For curious individuals wanting to learn more about the great state of Idaho, this series will bring the secrets of our state alive for all to appreciate and enjoy.

Stan Steiner, Ph.D.
Series Editor

Office of the Governor • First Lady Lori Otter • P.O. Box 83720
Boise, ID 83720-0034 • (208) 334-2100 • firstlady.idaho.gov

The Lori and Butch Otter Pre K-12 Idaho Education Series
Boise State University Publications Office • 1910 University Drive
Boise, ID 83725-1135 • (208) 426-1514
books@boisestate.edu • www.booksboisestate.com

Lori J. Otter
First Lady of Idaho

Ward Hooper
Artist

Bob Evancho
Writer/Editor

Adele Thomsen
Boise State University
Graphic Designer/Art Director

Todd Shallat, Ph.D.
Boise State University
Consulting Editor

Dan Chadwick
Idaho Association of Counties
Editorial Consultant

Corinn Evancho, Joe H. Evancho, Sue Evancho and **Kelly Roberts**
Technical Assistants

Greetings and Welcome to Ida Tours the 44

As you travel Idaho's streets and highways, you will notice that most of the license plates on the cars and other vehicles from our state begin with a number and a letter or just a single letter. We know that those numbers and letters tell us what county that vehicle is from. For example, the plates on a car from Twin Falls County (where my hometown is located) will be 2T because Twin Falls is the second county that begins with the letter "T." An automobile with the letter "K"on its plates is from Kootenai County, the only county that starts with "K."

Governor C.L. "Butch" Otter and First Lady Lori Otter with JC (age 10), Kenny (1), Greta (3), Ruby (6) and Emma (2).

As an Idaho teacher, I thought those license plates would be a great visual way to teach students about our state's geography. Idaho is a big state, the 14th-largest in the United States with 82,751 square miles. It also has many amazing natural features that make each of our 44 counties unique. *Ida Tours the 44* is a book that will teach you about what makes each county a very special part of Idaho.

Who better to take you on a tour of our state than our friend Ida? Ida is the main character in this series' first book, *Ida Visits the Capitol*. She is the barnstorming pilot of Idaho's past who flies back in time to share a journey of historical discovery. This time Ida's adventures take her back and forth across the state several times as she visits each county in alphabetical order and shares information on each one during her stops.

In her flight plan, Ida will use each county seat's coordinates (latitude, longitude and elevation) to help her locate each runway. While she is airborne, Ida will use Idaho's many geographical formations and man-made landmarks—our mountains, rivers, deserts, cities, bridges, forests, canyons, dams and lakes—to help navigate her way back and forth across the Gem State.

Each county profile contains a brainteaser about that county. One red letter from each of the answers is part of a puzzle answer. Complete the letter clues with the 44 red letters to decode the puzzle in the back of the book. Ida's journey to each county certainly is not the most direct route, but it will give us an enjoyable opportunity to learn about many of the diverse, wondrous and fascinating places in our state.

Governor Otter and I wish you a safe flight with our friend Ida; we know you are in safe hands. We hope you have an informative and fun-filled journey learning about the state we love so much and the wonders of each of Idaho's 44 counties.

Lori Jean Otter

Lori J. Otter
First Lady of Idaho

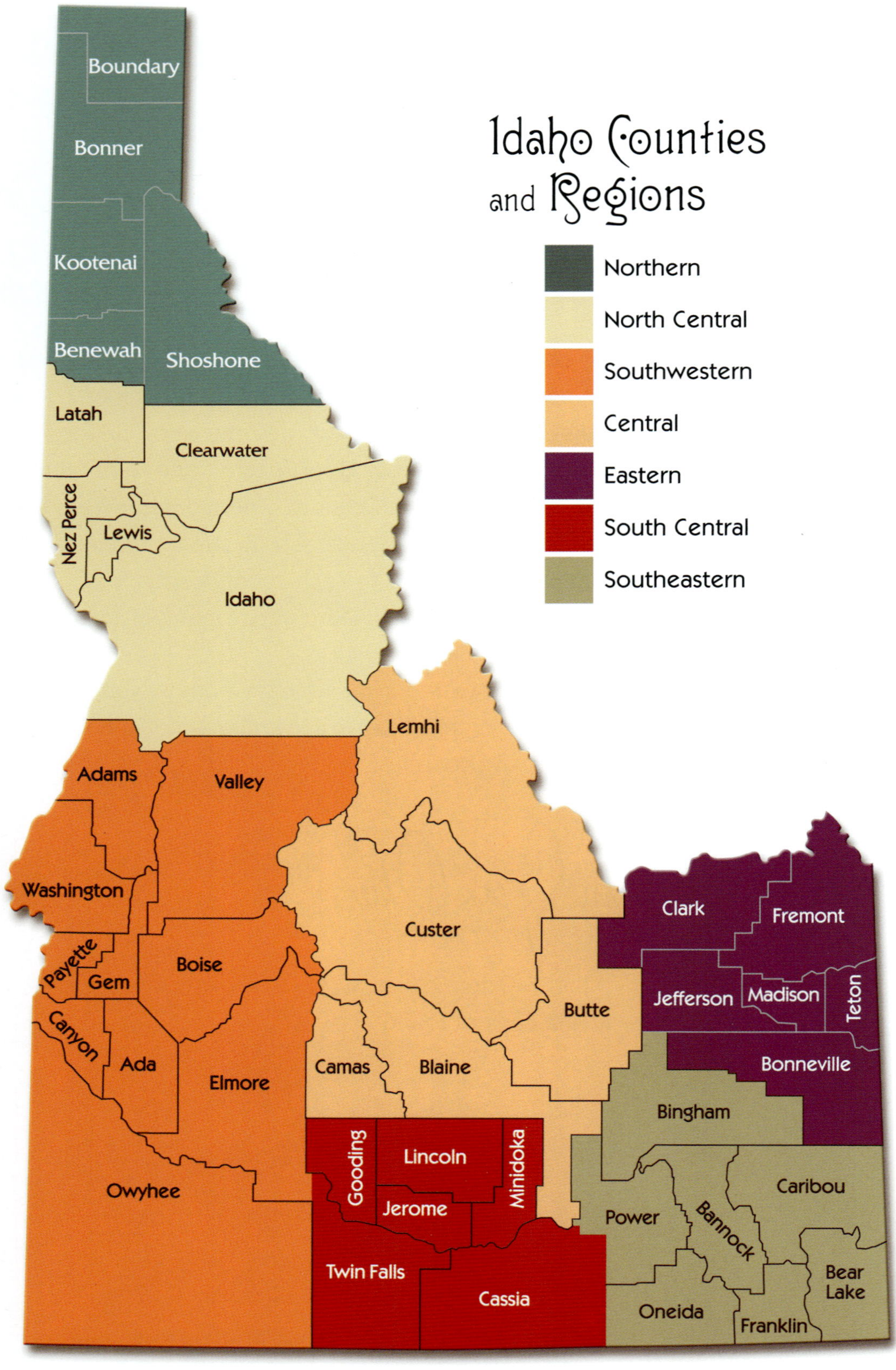
Idaho Counties
and Regions
Northern
North Central
Southwestern
Central
Eastern
South Central
Southeastern
Boundary
Bonner
Kootenai
Benewah
Shoshone
Latah
Clearwater
Nez Perce
Lewis
Idaho
Lemhi
Adams
Valley
Washington
Custer
Clark
Fremont
Payette
Gem
Boise
Butte
Jefferson
Madison
Teton
Canyon
Ada
Elmore
Camas
Blaine
Bonneville
Bingham
Gooding
Lincoln
Minidoka
Jerome
Owyhee
Power
Bannock
Caribou
Twin Falls
Cassia
Oneida
Franklin
Bear Lake

Complete the Puzzle

Each county profile contains a brainteaser about that county. One "red" letter from each of the answers is part of a puzzle, but what does it mean? Find out by completing the words to the puzzle in the back of the book with the 44 red letters.

A federal experimental facility in Clark County conducts research on these domestic animals.

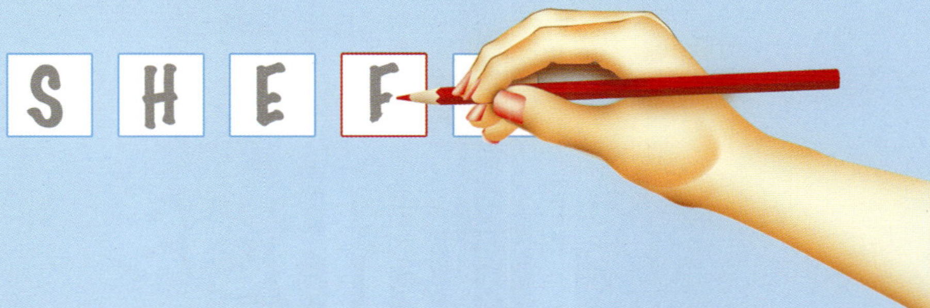

Note: On the following pages, distances between counties and elevations and latitudes/longitudes are based on county seats. Elevations are feet above sea level at county seats. Latitude is degrees north of the equator; longitude is degrees west of the prime meridian.

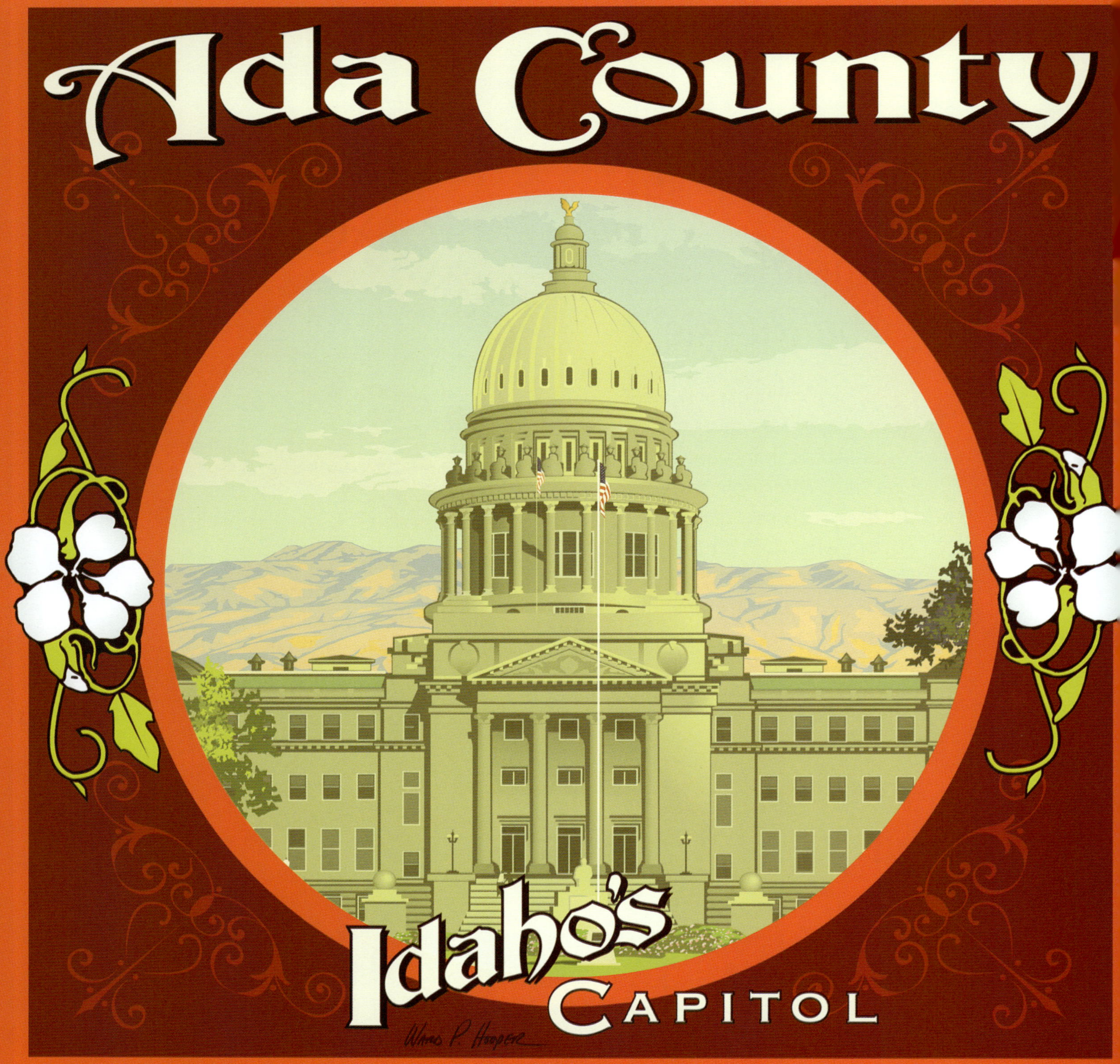

Cities and towns: Boise, Eagle, Garden City, Kuna, Meridian and Star

IDAHO 1A Office of the Governor

- **Established**: 1864
- **Named for**: Ada Riggs, daughter of Idaho territorial leader and Boise city co-founder H.C. Riggs
- **County seat**: Boise
- **Area**: 1,055 square miles
- **Elevation**: 2,842 feet
- **Latitude and longitude**: 43.60 degrees north; 116.22 degrees west

About the same size as Rhode Island, Ada County has the largest population of all the counties in Idaho. Most Ada County residents live in Boise, Idaho's state capital and largest city. Meridian is also one of Idaho's largest and fastest-growing cities. Boise, Meridian and the nearby cities of Eagle, Kuna and Garden City combine to make Ada County the largest urban area in our state. Among the buildings that line the busy streets of downtown Boise is Idaho's Capitol. With elegant columns and a dome that rises more than 200 feet from the ground floor, Idaho's Capitol looks similar to our nation's Capitol in Washington, D.C. Ada County is also the home of Boise State University, Idaho's largest college. Among Ada County's many attractions is the Boise Greenbelt, a pathway that lines the banks of the Boise River and connects a dozen parks for walkers, bikers, runners, wildlife observers and fishermen. Ada County has thousands of acres of public land that is home to wildlife, plants and historic landmarks. **Next stop**: Seventy-eight miles north along the western fringe of the Boise National Forest and the western shore of Cascade Reservoir to Adams County.

Brainstorm

Located in Ada County, this is Idaho's largest city and state capital.

Cities and towns: Council, Fruitvale, Indian Valley, Meadows, Mesa and New Meadows

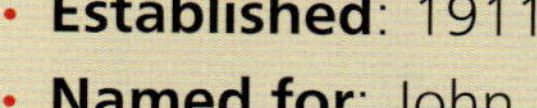

- **Established**: 1911
- **Named for**: John Adams, second president of the United States
- **County seat**: Council
- **Area**: 1,376 square miles
- **Elevation:** 2,927 feet
- **Latitude and longitude**: 44.72 degrees north; 116.43 degrees west

Adams County is among the most scenic of Idaho's 44 counties. It has rugged mountains, thick forests, flowing rivers and high desert areas. It is bordered on the west by Hells Canyon, North America's deepest river gorge. Also in Adams County is Sheep Rock National Natural Landmark, a large field of volcanic rock in the Payette National Forest. In the late 1930s Adams County had a booming timber industry. Fifty years later, however, its lumber business began to decline and the last sawmill in the county seat of Council closed in 1995. Early in the 20th century the town of Mesa had one of the largest orchards in the world with 1,200 acres of various fruit trees, mostly apples. The original residents of Adams County were small bands of Shoshone Indians, and the Council Valley was a meeting place for the Shoshone and Nez Perce tribes. Settlers arrived in the 19th century. **Next stop**: Ida takes off on a 237-mile flight heading southeast over the Boise National Forest, the Sawtooth Mountains, Craters of the Moon National Monument and Preserve and the Snake River Plain to Bannock County.

Brainstorm

Located on the western border of Adams County, this is North America's deepest river gorge.

Cities and towns: Arimo, Chubbuck, Downey, Inkom, Lava Hot Springs, McCammon and Pocatello

- **Established**: 1893
- **Named for**: Native American tribe
- **County seat**: Pocatello
- **Area**: 1,113 square miles
- **Elevation**: 4,365 feet
- **Latitude and longitude**: 42.87 degrees north; 112.46 degrees west

The early railroads of the American West put Bannock County on the map. During the days after the Oregon Trail, the town of Pocatello became one of the largest railway centers in the West. Bannock and Shoshone Native American tribes inhabited Bannock County for hundreds of years before settlers arrived.

Today the Fort Hall Indian Reservation is split between northern Bannock County and southern Bingham County. Fort Hall is also a national historic landmark because of the important role it played in the 1860s and 1870s as a connection for the overland stage, mail and freight lines to towns and camps of the mining frontier in the Pacific Northwest. Pocatello is the county seat of Bannock County and one of Idaho's largest cities. With the use of irrigation from the nearby Snake River, Bannock County is a major supplier and producer of potatoes, grain and other crops. With its numerous public hot springs, the city of Lava Hot Springs is a popular resort location. Bannock County is also the home of Idaho State University. **Next stop**: A short 68-mile hop to the southeast over the Caribou-Targhee National Forest and into Bear Lake County.

Brainstorm

Part of this Indian reservation is in Bannock County.

Cities and towns: Bloomington, Fish Haven, Georgetown, Montpelier, Ovid, Paris and St. Charles

- **Established**: 1893
- **Named for**: Lake on Idaho-Utah border
- **County seat**: Paris
- **Area**: 971 square miles
- **Elevation**: 5,968 feet
- **Latitude and longitude**: 42.22 degrees north; 111.40 degrees west

Located in Idaho's southeast corner, Bear Lake County is named after the large and beautiful lake at its southern end. Twenty miles long and 8 miles wide, Bear Lake is a popular spot for boaters, water skiers, swimmers and fishermen. Located near Montpelier, Bear Lake National Wildlife Refuge contains 19,000 acres of marsh, open water and grasslands that provide nesting areas for various waterfowl. The county is also well known for its cattle ranches and grain farms. Bear Lake County is also the home of Minnetonka Cave, the largest limestone rock cave in Idaho. The cave has a half-mile route lined with stalactites and stalagmites. Native Americans recognized what is now Bear Lake County as prime hunting grounds, and the area was a frequent camping area for traveling bands of the Shoshone, Ute and Bannock tribes. Bear Lake was originally named Black Bear Lake because many black bears roamed the area. **Next stop**: A 432-mile trip heading northwest as Ida soars over the Arco Desert, flies between the Lost River and Lemhi mountain ranges, over the Salmon-Challis and Nez Perce national forests and lands in Benewah County.

Brainstorm

These limestone deposits can be found in Minnetonka Cave in Bear Lake County.

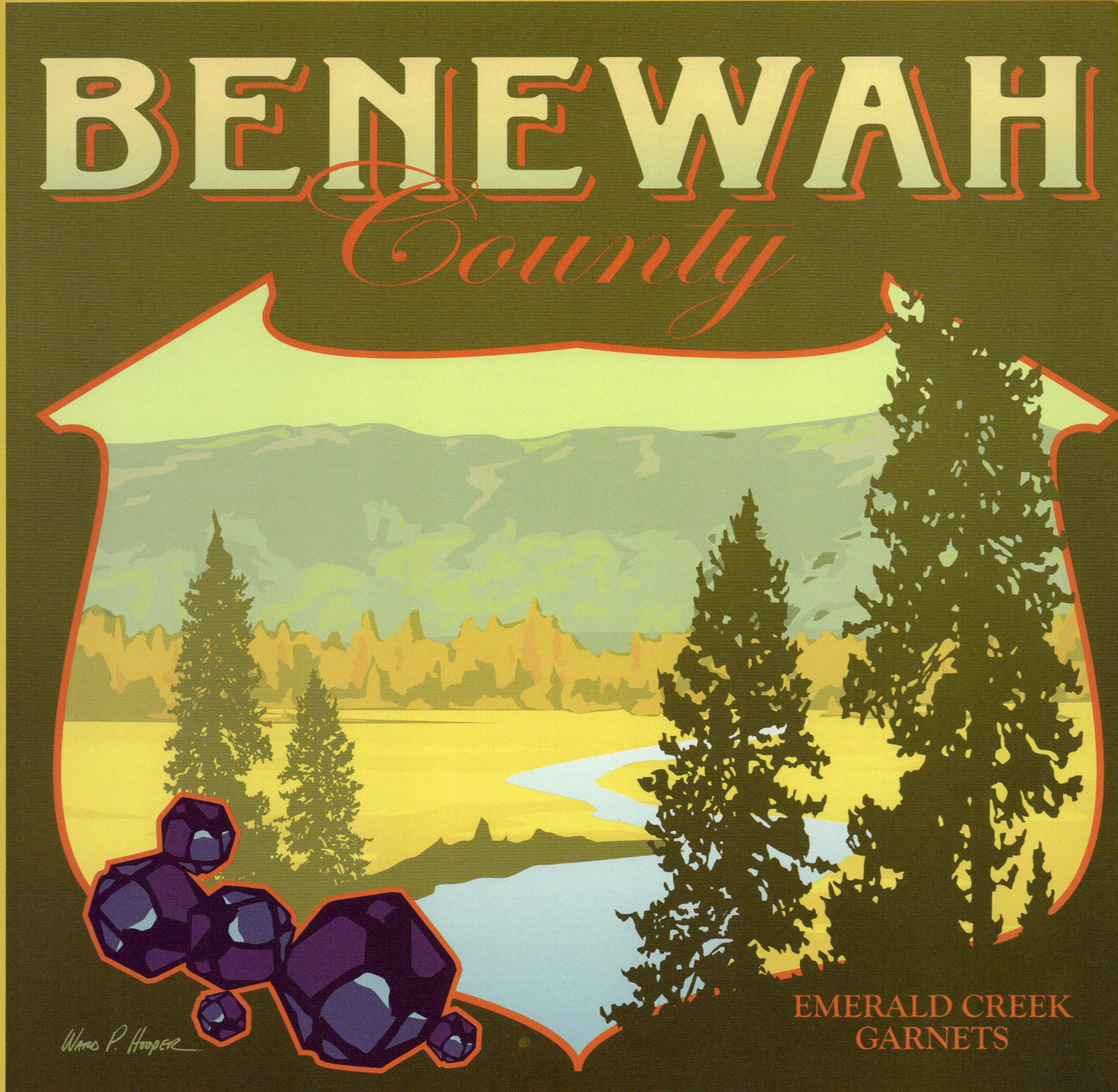

Cities and towns: Parkline, Plummer, St. Maries and Tensed

northern 3B benewah

- **Established**: 1915
- **Named for**: Chief of Coeur d'Alene Native American tribe
- **County seat**: St. Maries
- **Area**: 776 square miles
- **Elevation**: 2,216 feet
- **Latitude and longitude**: 47.31 degrees north; 116.57 degrees west

Benewah County is among our state's most scenic areas. Located in a forested valley that includes the St. Joe and St. Maries rivers and the lower portion of Lake Coeur d'Alene, the county's primary industries are agriculture, logging and tourism. The St. Joe River Valley in Benewah County is considered one of the finest elk hunting areas in the United States. Adding to the area's natural beauty is Heyburn State Park, the oldest park in the Pacific Northwest. Established in 1908, Heyburn features tall ponderosa pines that tower over grassy hillsides. Benewah County is also the home of Emerald Creek Garnet Area. Emerald Creek and India are the only two places in the world where the rare gemstone known as the star garnet can be found. Benewah County was a gathering place for the Coeur d'Alene Native American tribe. Some settlement began in 1860, but most homesteaders came to the area after the discovery of gold near St. Maries in 1880. **Next stop**: A 351-mile trip heading southeast over north Idaho's Dworshak Reservoir and flying above the Selway-Bitterroot Wilderness Area and the Lemhi Mountain Range to Bingham County.

Brainstorm

Emerald Creek in Benewah County is just one of two places in the world where this rare gemstone can be found.

Cities and towns: Aberdeen, Atomic City, Basalt, Blackfoot, Firth, Moreland, Pingree, Riverside, Rockford, Shelley, Springfield and Sterling

- **Established**: 1885
- **Named for**: Henry Bingham, Civil War general and Pennsylvania congressman
- **County seat**: Blackfoot
- **Area**: 2,095 square miles
- **Elevation**: 4,497 feet
- **Latitude and longitude**: 43.19 degrees north; 112.34 degrees west

Located on the eastern end of the Snake River Plain, Bingham County is the center of eastern Idaho's important potato industry. In fact, the county seat of Blackfoot is known as the Potato Capital of the World. Blackfoot is also the home of the Idaho Potato Museum. The Hell's Half Acre Lava Field is also located in Bingham County and neighboring Bonneville County. The 150-square-mile national natural landmark is a reminder of the volcanic activity that took place in Idaho about 5,200 years ago. While its main industry is agriculture, Bingham County is home to several businesses and State Hospital South, Idaho's largest mental health hospital. Bingham County was named after Henry Bingham. Who was he? Bingham was a congressman from Pennsylvania and a friend of William Bunn, who was Idaho's territorial governor when the county was established in 1885. As a young officer in the Civil War, Bingham rose from lieutenant to brigadier general and was awarded the Medal of Honor. **Next stop**: Ida takes a short 101-mile flight to the west, flying across the Snake River Plain and the Craters of the Moon National Monument and Preserve and landing in Blaine County.

Brainstorm

A museum in Bingham County is named for this world-famous Idaho crop.

Scenic BLAINE County

Cities and towns: Bellevue, Carey, Hailey, Ketchum, Picabo, Sun Valley and Triumph

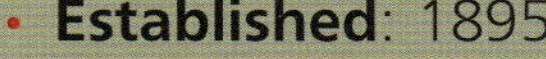

- **Established**: 1895
- **Named for**: James Blaine, U.S. secretary of state (1881 and 1889-1892)
- **County seat**: Hailey
- **Area**: 2,655 square miles
- **Elevation**: 5,330 feet
- **Latitude and longitude:** 43.51 degrees north; 114.29 degrees west

The world-famous Sun Valley Ski Resort is located in Blaine County. With its tall mountains and winding rivers and streams, Blaine County is one of the top outdoor recreation areas in the United States. In addition to downhill and cross-country skiing, activities such as kayaking, backpacking, hiking, golfing, swimming, horseback riding, mountain biking, camping and fishing bring thousands of tourists and recreation lovers from around the world to Blaine County year-round. The county's northern region holds the headwaters of the Salmon River, also known as the River of No Return. The Snake River Plain and Lake Walcott are found at the southern boundary of this odd-shaped county. The Sawtooth, Boulder, Smoky and Pioneer mountain ranges in Blaine County are among the most impressive in the nation. The Great Rift National Natural Landmark in the southeast portion of the county is similar to the landscape of the moon. Mining, sheep herding and farming were Blaine County's primary industries in the late 19th century before tourism took over with the building of the Sun Valley Resort in 1936. At one time Ketchum was one of the largest sheep shipping centers in the United States. **Next stop**: Ida takes a 79-mile hop northwest over the Sawtooth and Boise national forests to Boise County.

Brainstorm

Scenic mountains and some of the best skiing in North America are two reasons this is among Blaine County's top industries.

BOISE

Famous Gold Strike of 1862

Ward P. Hooper

COUNTY

Cities and towns: Banks, Centerville, Crouch, Garden Valley, Horseshoe Bend, Idaho City, Lowman, New Centerville, Pioneerville and Placerville

- **Established**: 1864
- **Named for**: Boise River
- **County seat**: Idaho City
- **Area**: 1,902 square miles
- **Elevation**: 3,906 feet
- **Latitude and longitude:** 43.84 degrees north; 115.85 degrees west

Boise County has a rich and lively history because of the gold rush that took place there in the 1860s and 1870s. When gold was discovered in Boise County in 1862, the area soon became home to approximately 25,000 people trying to strike it rich. The county's Boise Basin was one of the largest sources of gold ever found, and the county seat of Idaho City was one of the region's largest cities for a number of years. But when the gold ran out, the residents left as quickly as they came. Many of the old brick homes and businesses as well as the plank boardwalks from the pioneer era remain in Idaho City today. Bogus Basin ski area is in the southwestern part of Boise County, and the eastern area of the county contains the central section of the Sawtooth Wilderness. **Next stop**: A 492-mile flight heading north along the Middle Fork of the Payette River and the South Fork of the Salmon River, rising above the Salmon River and Clearwater Mountains, over the Coeur d'Alene and St. Joe national forests, and into Bonner County in Idaho's panhandle.

Brainstorm

This precious metal created a "rush" of prospectors and pioneers in the late 19th century in Boise County.

Cities and towns: Clark Fork, Hope, Oldtown, Ponderay, Priest River, Sagle and Sandpoint

northern 7B bonner

- **Established**: 1907
- **Named for**: Edwin Bonner, originator of an 1864 ferry service on the Kootenai River
- **County seat**: Sandpoint
- **Area**: 1,738 square miles
- **Elevation**: 2,070 feet
- **Latitude and longitude**: 48.27 degrees north; 116.55 degrees west

Lake Pend Oreille is located in Bonner County. Sixty-five miles long and covering 148 square miles, the lake is Idaho's largest. With depths down to 1,150 feet in some parts, it is also one of the deepest lakes in the United States. The lake was named for a local Indian tribe known for the pendants they wore in their earlobes. National forests and a few small towns surround Lake Pend Oreille, including the county seat of Sandpoint. Part of Priest Lake also lies in Bonner County's northwest corner. The Clark Fork, Pend Oreille and Priest rivers run through the county. The Selkirk Mountain Range sits on the western side of the county and the sharp-peaked Cabinet Mountains border the county on the east. Round Lake State Park is one of Bonner County's top tourist attractions. The park sits on 142 acres of forest that surrounds a 58-acre lake at an elevation of 2,122 feet. **Next stop**: A 522-mile flight that is one of Ida's longest as she heads southeast over the heart of Idaho's rugged wilderness, west of the Bitterroot Mountains and over the St. Joe, Clearwater, Nez Perce and Salmon-Challis national forests to Bonneville County.

Brainstorm

Located in Bonner County, this is Idaho's largest and one of America's deepest lakes.

Cities and towns: Ammon, Idaho Falls, Iona, Irwin, Swan Valley and Ucon

eastern 8B bonneville

- **Established**: 1911
- **Named for**: Benjamin Bonneville, French-born American West explorer
- **County seat**: Idaho Falls
- **Area**: 1,869 square miles
- **Elevation**: 4,742 feet
- **Latitude and longitude**: 43.49 degrees north; 112.03 degrees west

Eastern Idaho's regional center for health care, travel and business, Bonneville County has one of the largest metropolitan areas in Idaho. Bonneville County also has the most residents in eastern Idaho, and the county seat of Idaho Falls is one of the largest cities in our state. A popular tourist attraction is the waterfalls on the Snake River near downtown Idaho Falls. The falls drop 20 feet over a width of about 1,200 feet, creating a spectacular view from the Broadway Bridge and both sides of the river. Bonneville County's economy was mostly farming until the Atomic Energy Commission opened the National Reactor Testing Station in the Arco Desert about 60 miles west of Idaho Falls in 1949. Much of the county's economy became dependent on jobs from the nuclear site, which is now called the Idaho National Laboratory. The Museum of Idaho is located in Idaho Falls. The museum is dedicated to preserving and showcasing the natural and cultural history of Idaho. Bonneville County is also the home of Eastern Idaho Technical College, which started in 1969 as a vocational-technical college. **Next stop**: Ida's longest trip—a 604-mile flight northwest to Boundary County in Idaho's panhandle.

Brainstorm

The county seat of Bonneville County, this is one of the Gem State's largest cities.

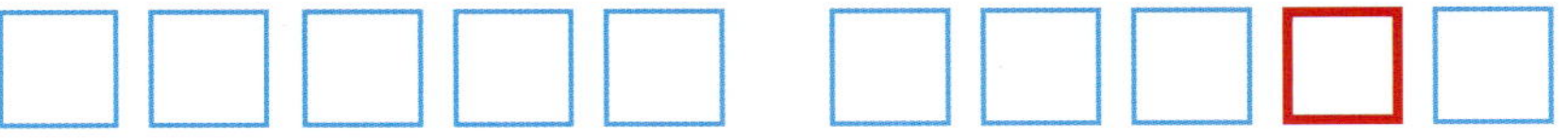

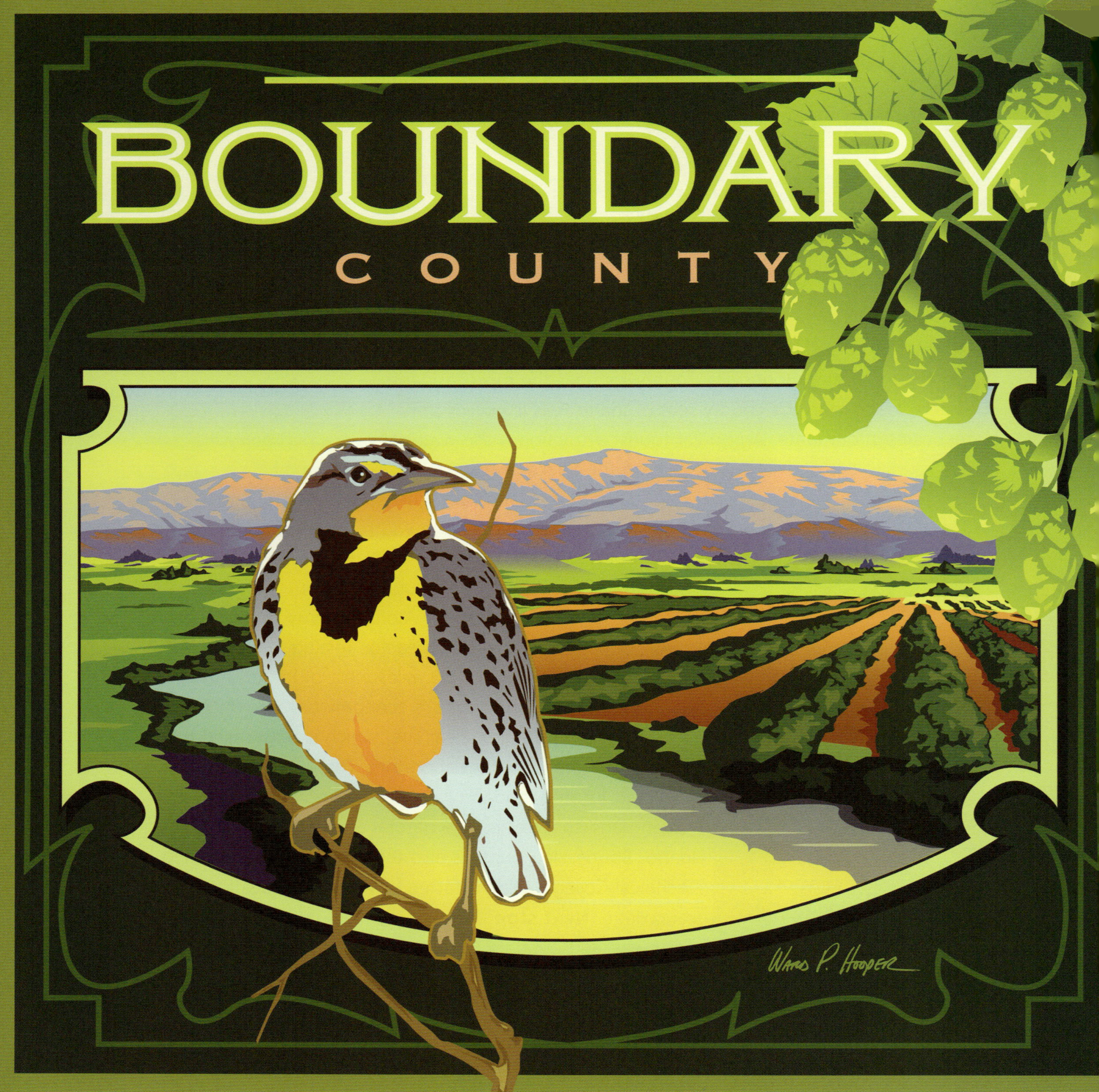

Cities and towns: Bonners Ferry, Eastport, Moyie Springs, Naples and Porthill

9B northern boundary

- **Established**: 1915
- **Named for**: Bordering Canada to the north
- **County seat**: Bonners Ferry
- **Area**: 1,269 square miles
- **Elevation**: 1,773 feet
- **Latitude and longitude**: 48.69 degrees north; 116.31 degrees west

How did Boundary County get its name? It's pretty simple: Idaho's northernmost county is bordered by Washington state on the west, Montana on the east and British Columbia, Canada, on the north. The county seat of Bonners Ferry was a fur-trading post established in 1808 by local trappers, but a permanent settlement was not made until 1864. Pioneer Edwin Bonner built a ferry that replaced the Indian canoes that had ferried miners and other explorers across the Kootenai River to the Canadian gold fields. Kootenai Wildlife Refuge and Priest Lake State Park are among the county's top attractions. Priest Lake State Park is on the eastern shore of the 19-mile long, 300-foot deep lake of the same name. Every year the park draws hundreds of tourists and outdoor enthusiasts who visit to fish, hunt, hike, camp, canoe, kayak, snowmobile and mountain bike. The 2,774-acre Kootenai Wildlife Refuge was established in 1965 to provide important habitat for migrating waterfowl. Boundary County is also surrounded by the Selkirk, Purcell and Cabinet mountain ranges. **Next stop**: Ida heads 378 miles southeast over the rugged wilderness of central Idaho, over the Lost River Mountain Range and Borah Peak, landing in Butte County.

Brainstorm

This Canadian province borders Boundary County to the north.

☐☐☐☐☐☐☐ ☐☐☐☐☐☐☐☐

BUTTE COUNTY

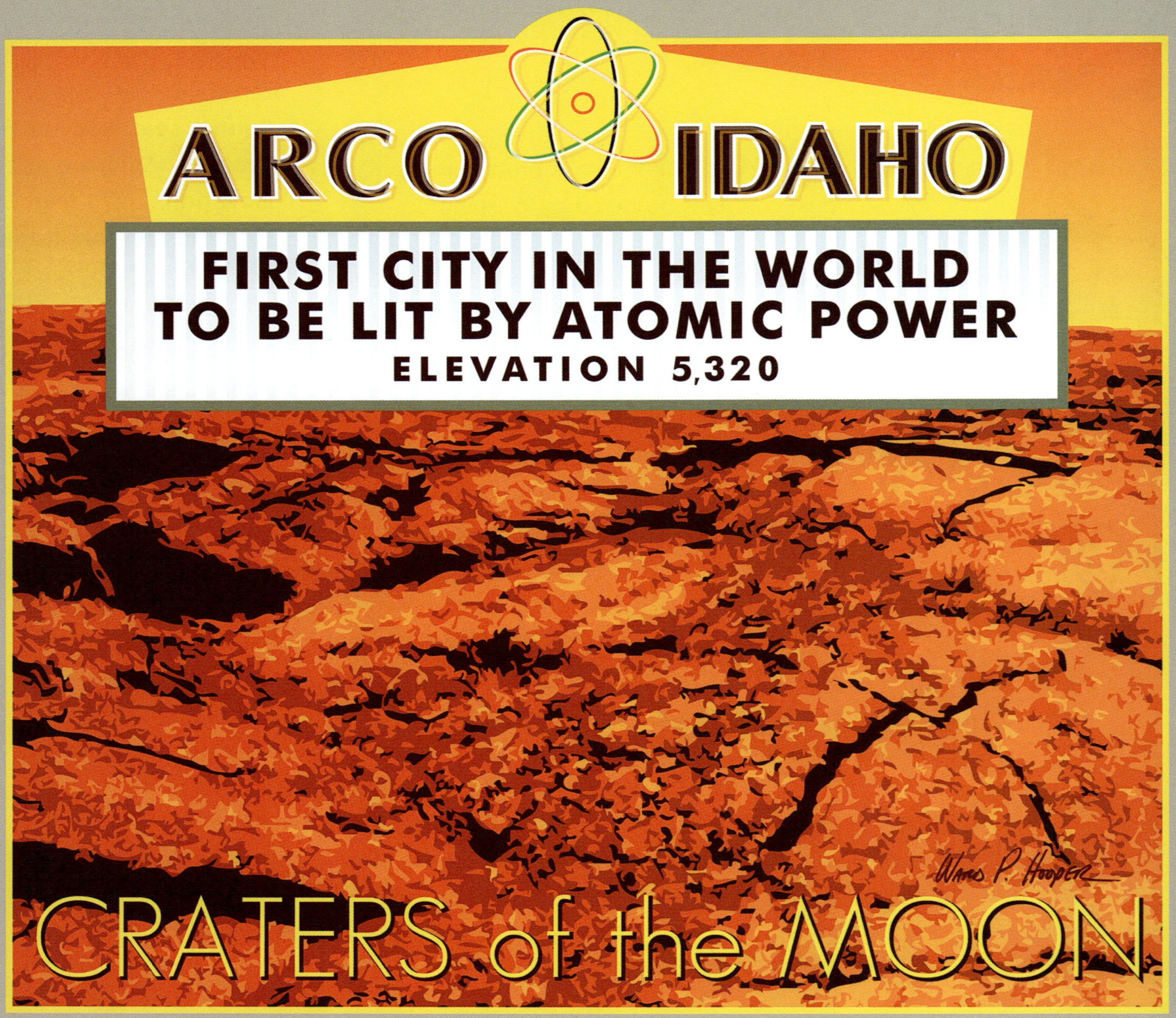

Cities and towns: Arco, Butte City, Darlington, Howe and Moore

central 10B butte

- **Established**: 1917
- **Named for**: Buttes rising from the Snake River Plain
- **County seat**: Arco
- **Area**: 2,233 square miles
- **Elevation**: 5,320 feet
- **Latitude and longitude**: 43.63 degrees north;113.29 degrees west

Butte County was named for the volcanic buttes that rise from the Snake River Plain and served as landmarks to trappers and pioneers who traveled through the area. The largest is the 2,500-foot Big Southern Butte in the southern part of the county. The Little Lost River is located in Butte County. Its waters disappear underground into the Snake River Plain Aquifer to emerge 200 miles away in the Hagerman Valley at Thousand Springs. The southwestern portion of the county includes the visitor center at the Craters of the Moon National Monument and Preserve, which extends south and west into three other counties. Craters of the Moon contains three major lava fields that cover almost half a million acres. Much of the eastern part of Butte County contains the vast Idaho National Laboratory, which extends eastward into neighboring counties. On July 17, 1955, Arco used the nuclear power produced by INL to become the first city in the world to be lighted by atomic power. Butte County is also the home of Experimental Breeder Reactor, a national historic landmark that produced the first usable electricity to be created by nuclear power. **Next stop**: A 76-mile trip west over Blaine County to Camas County.

Brainstorm

This national monument in Butte County is famous for its lava beds, which are similar to the lunar surface.

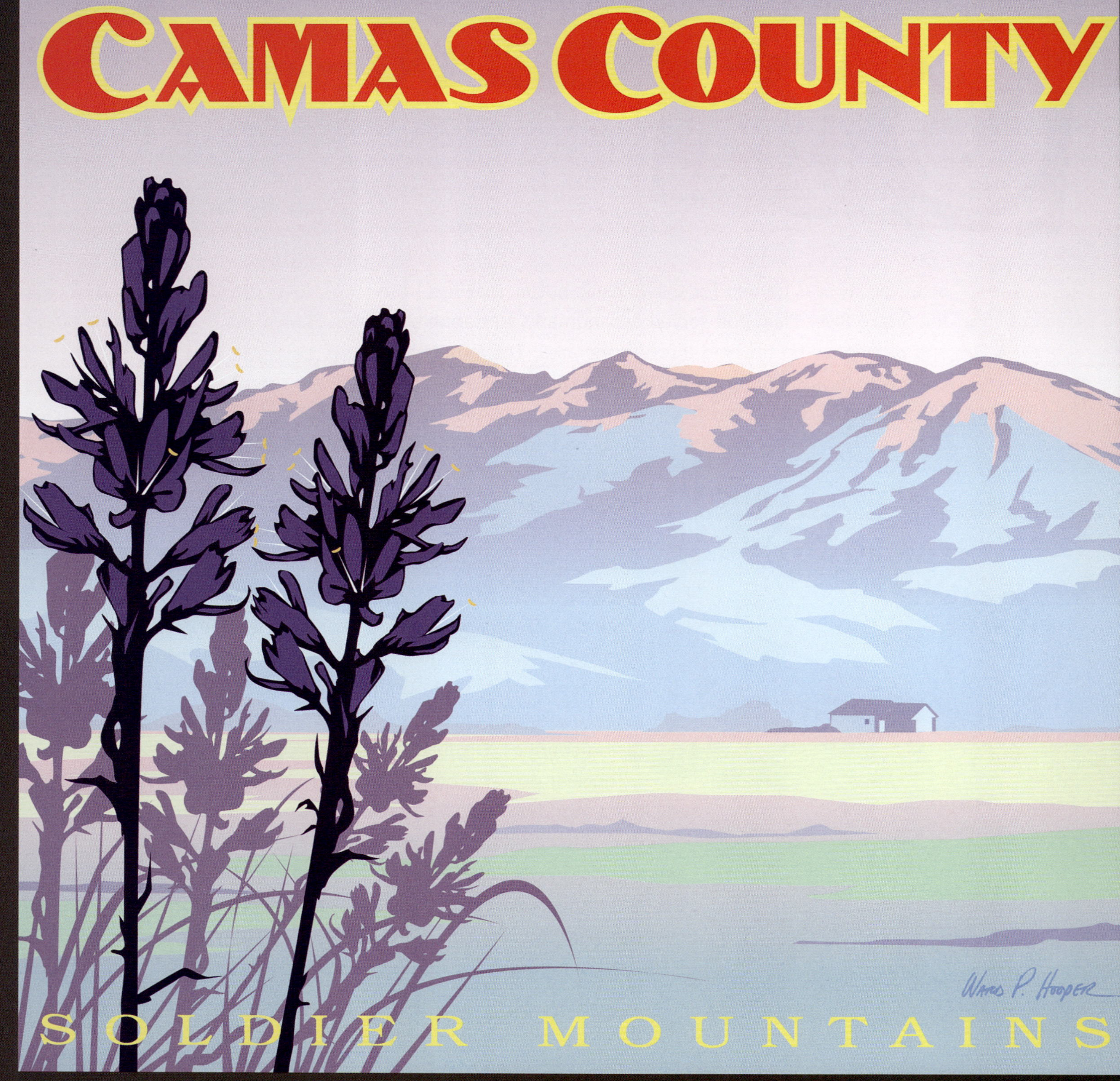

Cities and towns: Corral, Fairfield and Hill City

central 1C camas

- **Established**: 1917
- **Named for**: Camassia, a plant species important as a food source among Native Americans and early white settlers
- **County seat**: Fairfield
- **Area**: 1,075 square miles
- **Elevation**: 5,065 feet
- **Latitude and longitude**: 43.34 degrees north; 114.79 degrees west

Camas County is one of the most sparsely populated counties in Idaho. Spanning the center of the county is the Camas Prairie—a high plateau valley with an average elevation of 5,000 feet. Approximately 125,000 acres of the prairie are devoted to crops and pasture. Antelope, deer and other wildlife roam the prairie. Near the Bennett Hills on the west end of the county is the Camas Prairie Centennial Marsh Wildlife Management Area. The area covers just over 3,100 acres and provides a sanctuary for water-fowl, shorebirds and other wildlife. Camas County's wide-open spaces make it an ideal setting for many recreational opportunities, including hunting, fishing, skiing, snowboarding, hiking and camping. The Soldier Mountain ski area is 12 miles north of the county seat of Fairfield, and the world-famous Sun Valley Ski Resort is less than 50 miles away. The western end of Idaho's Magic Reservoir is 20 miles east of Fairfield. The Soldier and Smoky mountains of the Sawtooth National Forest are north of Fairfield. The highest point in Camas County is Two Point Mountain at 10,124 feet in the north-western section of the county. **Next stop**: Ninety-eight miles due west to Canyon County.

Brainstorm

Camas County was named for this plant species, which was a food source for its early occupants.

Cities and towns: Caldwell, Greenleaf, Melba, Middleton, Nampa, Notus, Parma and Wilder

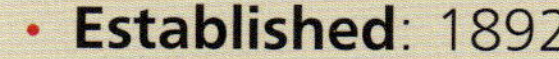

- **Established**: 1892
- **Named for**: Canyon of the Boise River near Caldwell and canyon of the Snake River, which forms part of the county's boundary
- **County seat**: Caldwell
- **Area**: 590 square miles
- **Elevation**: 2,367 feet
- **Latitude and longitude**: 43.65 degrees north; 116.67 degrees west

Only five Idaho counties are smaller in size, but Canyon County is one of the Gem State's largest in population. Along with neighboring Ada County, Canyon County is part of the Treasure Valley, one of the biggest metropolitan areas in the Pacific Northwest. Nampa and the county seat of Caldwell are two of Idaho's largest cities. While farming and ranching remain an important part of the county's economy, many high-tech companies and retail businesses have moved into the area because of its significant population growth. The Deer Flat National Wildlife Refuge is in Canyon County. The College of Idaho, Northwest Nazarene University and the College of Western Idaho are also in the county. Many early pioneers who traveled the Oregon Trail into the region decided to settle in the area and began farming in the Treasure Valley. In the 1880s Canyon County became a Union Pacific railway center and one of the most densely populated sections of Idaho. **Next stop**: Ida takes off and flies east over the Snake River Plain, begins her descent near American Falls Reservoir and lands 265 miles later in southeast Idaho's Caribou County.

Brainstorm

Canyon County is part of this urban area, the largest in the Gem State.

Cities and towns: Bancroft, Conda, Freedom, Grace, Henry, Soda Springs and Wayan

- **Established**: 1919
- **Named for**: Caribou Mountains
- **County seat**: Soda Springs
- **Area**: 1,799 square miles
- **Elevation**: 5,777 feet
- **Latitude and longitude**: 42.65 degrees north; 111.58 degrees west

Caribou County's Soda Springs is both the oldest and the youngest county seat in Idaho. How is that possible? In 1864 the Idaho Legislature created Oneida County and designated Soda Springs its county seat (the oldest). Three years later Oneida County moved its county seat to Malad City. In February of 1919, 55 years later, the Legislature created Caribou County and made Soda Springs its county seat (the youngest). A portion of Grays Lake National Wildlife Refuge is in Caribou County. The site has 18,330 acres of high-mountain marshland at the foot of the Caribou Mountains and provides breeding habitat for more than 200 species of mammals, birds, fish and amphibians. Grays Lake Refuge has the largest nesting population of greater sandhill cranes in the world and also provides nesting areas for Canada geese, ducks, gulls and white-faced ibis. Beginning in the 1830s Caribou County was on the routes of the earliest explorers, fur trappers and Oregon Trail pioneers. Thousands of pioneers passed through the present site of Soda Springs, named for the many natural springs in the area. **Next stop**: A 112-mile hop southwest to Cassia County.

Brainstorm

The Grays Lake National Wildlife Refuge in Caribou County has the largest nesting population in the world for this kind of bird.

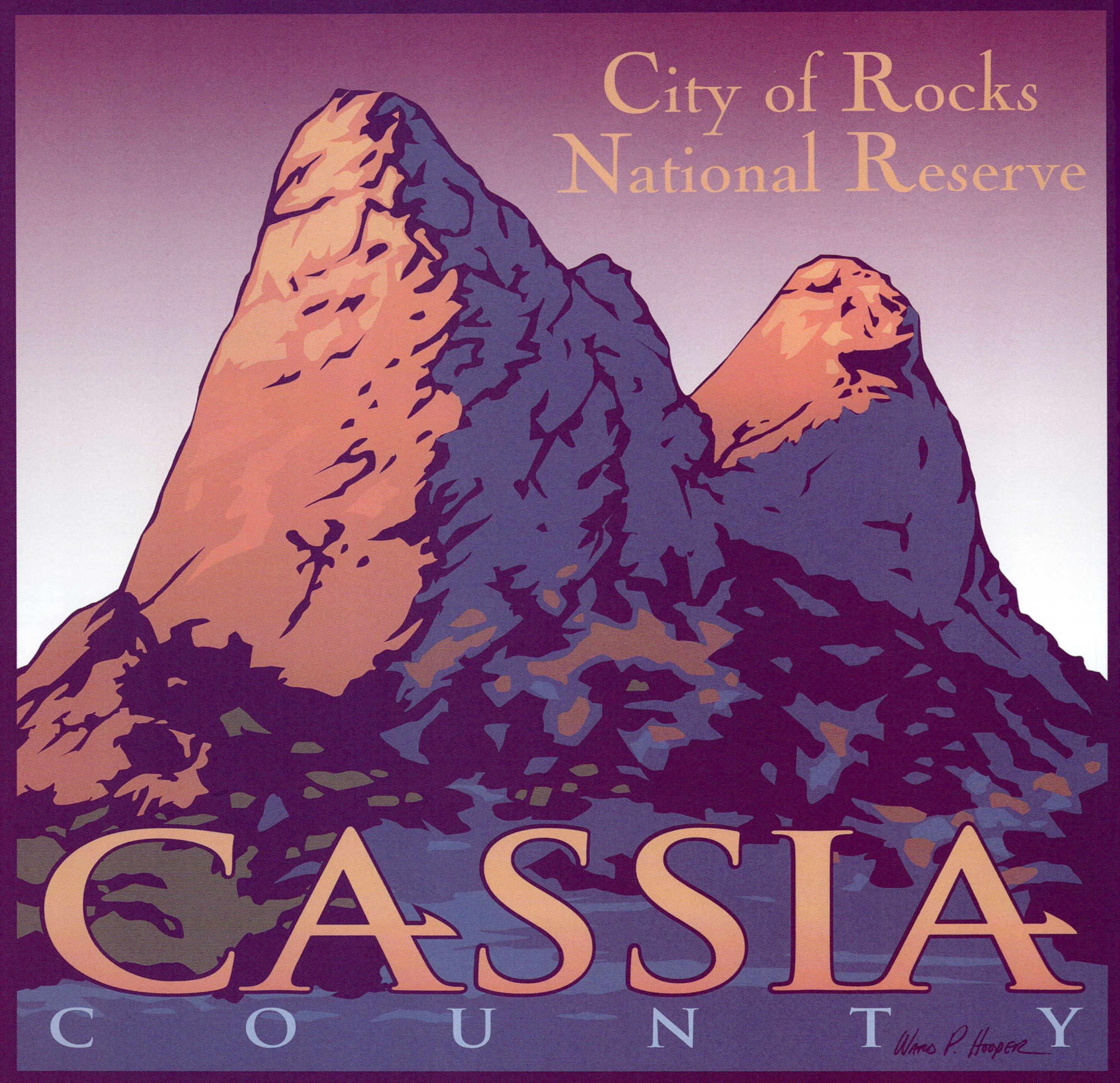

Cities and towns: Albion, Almo, Burley, Declo, Elba, Malta, Oakley and Sublett

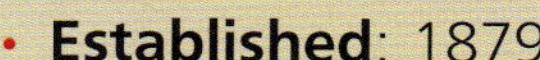

- **Established**: 1879
- **Named for**: Cassia Creek
- **County seat**: Burley
- **Area**: 2,567 square miles
- **Elevation**: 4,165 feet
- **Latitude and longitude**: 42.53 degrees north; 113.78 degrees west

Cassia County is on the Snake River Plain and part of southern Idaho's Magic Valley. The area was named "Magic" because of its conversion from desert to farmland using irrigation water from the Snake River. Larger than either Delaware or Rhode Island, Cassia County has several mountain ranges, including the Albion, Cotterel and Jim Sage mountains. Some of Idaho's most dramatic geological landforms are in Cassia County's Castle Rocks State Park and City of Rocks National Reserve. The 1,440-acre Castle Rocks area contains granite spires and monoliths. City of Rocks still bears the evidence of hundreds of pioneer inscriptions and wagon ruts left by the nearly quarter-million people who traveled through the area between 1843 and 1869 on the California Trail.

City of Rocks encompasses 14,407 acres of federal, state and private lands. The first people to inhabit Cassia County were the Paleo Indians. They settled in the area 15,000 to 16,000 years ago. The Shoshone, Paiute and Bannock tribes would later establish communities in the area using the natural resources of the land to hunt, fish and gather food. **Next stop**: Ida heads 138 miles northeast over the eastern part of the Snake River Plain to Clark County.

Brainstorm

The Castle Rocks area in Cassia County contains spires and monoliths of this kind of rock.

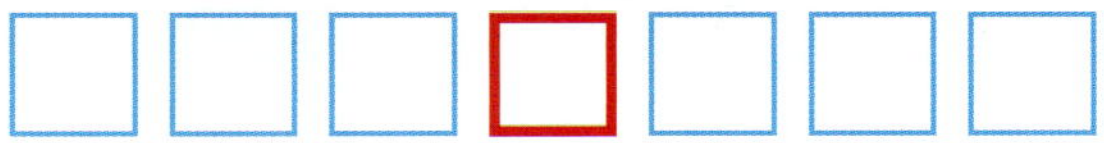

Cities and towns: Dubois, Kilgore and Spencer

- **Established**: 1919
- **Named for**: Sam Clark, early settler and member of Idaho Senate
- **County seat**: Dubois
- **Area**: 1,765 square miles
- **Elevation**: 5,148 feet
- **Latitude and longitude**: 44.17 degrees north; 112.22 degrees west

Less than 50 miles west of Yellowstone National Park, Clark County is one of the most sparsely populated and rustic counties in Idaho. Clark County's northern border is the Bitterroot Range of the Rocky Mountains, which forms part of the Continental Divide and the state line with Montana. The Continental Divide is a series of mountain ridges that extends from Alaska to Mexico and separates the water that flows into the Atlantic Ocean or Gulf of Mexico from the water that flows into the Pacific Ocean. The Camas Meadows Battle Sites National Historic Landmark near the town of Kilgore commemorates the fight between U.S. troops and Nez Perce warriors in 1877. Six miles north of the county seat of Dubois is the U.S. Sheep Experiment Station, which studies domestic sheep. Clark County's rugged and unpopulated terrain provides an ideal habitat for upland game birds such as sage grouse. Clark County is named for Sam Clark, an early settler who became the first state senator from the area. **Next stop**: A 252-mile northwesterly flight between the Bitterroot and Lemhi mountain ranges, over the Salmon-Challis and Nez Perce national forests, east of the Clearwater Mountains, into northern Idaho and Clearwater County.

Brainstorm

A federal experimental facility in Clark County conducts research on these domestic animals.

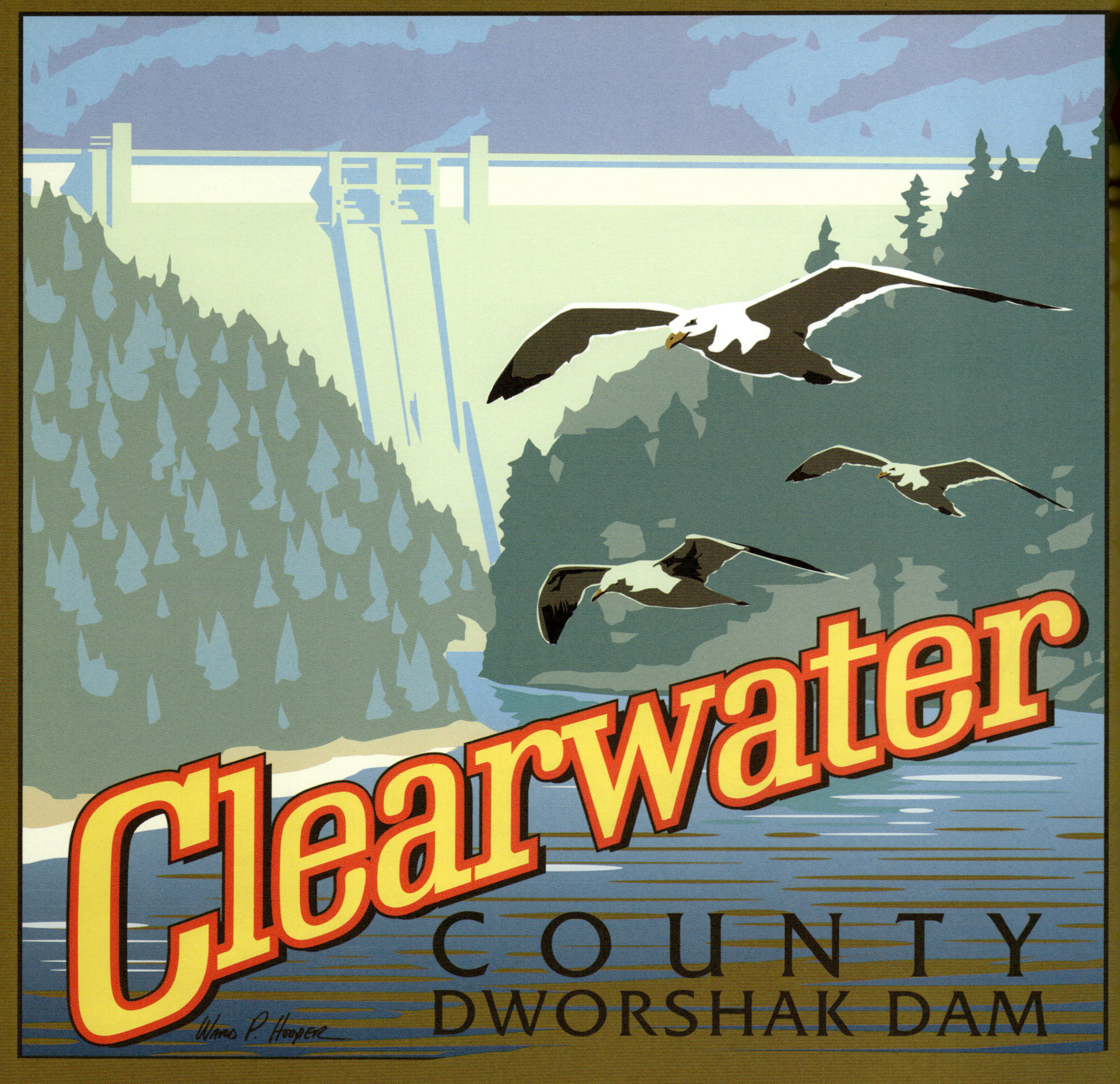

Cities and towns: Elk River, Orofino, Pierce and Weippe

6C north central clearwater

- **Established**: 1911
- **Named for**: Clearwater River
- **County seat**: Orofino
- **Area**: 2,462 square miles
- **Elevation**: 1,027 feet
- **Latitude and longitude**: 46.48 degrees north; 116.25 degrees west

Long before the Lewis and Clark Expedition passed through the area in 1805, what is now Clearwater County was home to Nez Perce Indians. The Nez Perce fed the hungry travelers and helped them build canoes at Canoe Camp, west of what is now the county seat of Orofino. Both the Clearwater River and the Lolo Pass in the southeast corner of the county were made famous by Lewis and Clark. Less than 70 years later, gold miners arrived in what is now the town of Pierce to establish northern Idaho's first white settlement. Built in 1862, the Pierce Courthouse is Idaho's oldest public building. Clearwater County's Lolo Trail and the Weippe Prairie are listed as national historic landmarks. From steep river canyons to high mountains, Clearwater County features a wide variety of terrains. Clearwater County is the home of the Dworshak Dam, the third-highest dam in the United States. Also in the county are the Dworshak Reservoir, Dworshak State Park and Dworshak National Fish Hatchery.

Next stop: Taking off and going west of the Clearwater Mountains, Ida flies 168 miles south over the Salmon-Challis National Forest and the Frank Church River of No Return Wilderness to Custer County.

Brainstorm

This dam in Clearwater County is the third-highest in the United States.

The County Of

CUSTER

Cities and towns: Challis, Clayton, Mackay and Stanley

central 7C custer

- **Established**: 1881
- **Named for**: General Custer Mine, named after George Custer, U.S. Army general
- **County seat**: Challis
- **Area**: 4,926 square miles
- **Elevation**: 5,553 feet
- **Latitude and longitude**: 44.50 degrees north; 114.22 degrees west

Mountainous Custer County is our state's fourth-largest county in size, but it's also one of the smallest in population. Located in the center of Idaho, Custer County's landscape consists of arid desert, flat green valleys and rugged rocky peaks. The Lost River Range in the county includes Mount Borah. At 12,662 feet, it is the highest peak in the Gem State. The mountain is named for William Borah, who served in the U.S. Senate for Idaho from 1907-40. Custer County also contains much of the Frank Church River of No Return Wilderness and the Salmon River. On the western border of the county are Idaho's famous Sawtooth Mountains and Sawtooth National Recreation Area. The tallest mountain in the Sawtooths is Thompson Peak, which rises above scenic Redfish Lake. The White Cloud Mountains are also in Custer County. The highest elevation in the White Clouds is Castle Peak at 11,815 feet. Custer County also contains portions of the Salmon River, Pioneer and White Knob mountains. Ranching, mining and tourism are the county's main industries. **Next stop**: A 118-mile flight southwest over the Sawtooth National Forest and the eastern edge of Camas County to Elmore County.

Brainstorm

Named after a famous Idaho politician, this mountain in Custer County is the tallest peak in Idaho.

Cities and towns: Atlanta, Featherville, Glenns Ferry, Mountain Home and Pine

- **Established**: 1889
- **Named for**: Ida Elmore mines, noted for gold and silver production in the 1860s
- **County seat**: Mountain Home
- **Area**: 3,078 square miles
- **Elevation**: 3,143 feet
- **Latitude and longitude**: 43.13 degrees north; 115.68 degrees west

Three Island Crossing in Elmore County is the historic site of one of the most famous crossings of the Snake River on the Oregon Trail. Pioneers used the dangerous crossing until 1870 when a local resident named Gus Glenn built a ferry about two miles upstream near what is now the town that is named after him, Glenns Ferry. At the Oregon Trail History and Education Center near Glenns Ferry visitors can learn about the trail as well as Native American history. What is now the county seat of Mountain Home was originally called Rattlesnake and served as a station on the overland stage route. Elmore County is the home of Mountain Home Air Force Base. The base has nearly 4,000 active-duty men and women. The base opened in 1943 for bomber training during World War II. It became a fighter base in 1966. Anderson Ranch Dam on the South Fork of the Boise River is in Elmore County. When it was completed in 1950 it became the tallest dam of its type in the world. Its primary purposes are to provide irrigation water and hydroelectric power. **Next stop**: A 206-mile flight southeast across the Magic Valley to Franklin County.

Brainstorm

The largest city and county seat of Elmore County has the same name as this nearby military base.

Cities and towns: Clifton, Dayton, Franklin, Mink Creek, Oxford, Preston, Thatcher, Weston and Whitney

- **Established**: 1913
- **Named for**: Franklin Richards, early Mormon church apostle
- **County seat**: Preston
- **Area**: 666 square miles
- **Elevation**: 4,715 feet
- **Latitude and longitude**: 42.09 degrees north; 111.87 degrees west

Thirteen Mormon pioneer families founded the town of Franklin in 1860, making it the first permanent white settlement in Idaho. The first schoolhouse in Idaho was built in Franklin in 1861. The Bear River Massacre Site in Franklin County is a national historic landmark. The site commemorates a battle in 1863 between government soldiers and members of the Shoshone tribe. It was the bloodiest encounter between Native Americans and white men to take place in the West between 1848 and 1891. More than 300 Shoshone warriors and 14 soldiers were killed in the battle. Franklin County has 17 mountain summits and peaks. Andrew Nyman Mountain and Wilderness Peak are the county's two tallest mountains. Oxford Slough Waterfowl Production Area is in Franklin and Bannock counties. The area is mostly marsh, but it has some open water and cropland. Preston is the county seat and largest city. It is also the home of the popular Preston Night Rodeo, which began in 1934. Named after Franklin Richards, an apostle of the Mormon church, Franklin County is the only county in the United States with that name that is not named after Benjamin Franklin. **Next stop**: A 129-mile flight north to Fremont County.

Brainstorm

In 1863 a deadly battle between Shoshone warriors and U.S. soldiers took place at this site in Franklin County.

UPPER MESA FALLS

Fremont

COUNTY

Cities and towns: Ashton, Chester, Drummond, Island Park, Lamont, Mack's Inn, Marysville, Newdale, Parker, St. Anthony, Teton, Warm River and Wilford

- **Established**: 1893
- **Named for**: John Fremont, American West explorer
- **County seat**: St. Anthony
- **Area**: 1,867 square miles
- **Elevation**: 4,967 feet
- **Latitude and longitude**: 43.96 degrees north; 111.68 degrees west

Located on the southwest border of Yellowstone National Park, Fremont County welcomes thousands of tourists each year and is one of the most scenic of Idaho's 44 counties. Upper Mesa Falls measures 300 feet wide and drops more than 100 feet into Henry's Fork of the Snake River. Fremont County's Henry's Lake State Park and Harriman State Park and the surrounding areas have some of the best fishing in North America. Other scenic attractions include the Lower Mesa Falls, St. Anthony Sand Dunes, Island Park Reservoir and Big Springs National Natural Landmark. In 1893 Fremont County became the first county established in Idaho after the Gem State was admitted to the union three years earlier. One of the worst disasters in Idaho history occurred in Fremont County in June of 1976 when the Teton Dam collapsed. An estimated 80 billion gallons of water from the Teton River Canyon flooded parts of the Upper Snake River Valley, resulting in 11 deaths and hundreds of millions of dollars in property damage. The earthen dam was never rebuilt. **Next stop**: A straight shot 238 miles due west through the middle of the state to Gem County.

Brainstorm

In 1976 this man-made structure in Fremont County collapsed, causing one of the worst disasters in Idaho history.

Cities and towns: Emmett, Letha, Montour, Ola and Sweet

southwestern 1G gem

- **Established**: 1915
- **Named for**: State nickname of Gem State
- **County seat**: Emmett
- **Area**: 563 square miles
- **Elevation**: 2,375 feet
- **Latitude and longitude**: 43.87 degrees north; 116.49 degrees west

One of Idaho's smallest counties in size, Gem County has abundant outdoor recreational opportunities because of the Payette River. The river runs through the valley and provides irrigation water to thousands of acres of nearby farmland. In 1924 the federal government built the 183-foot-high Black Canyon Dam on the Payette River. The dam formed the 1,100-acre Black Canyon Reservoir, which has 12 miles of shoreline for boating and fishing. Started in the 1930s and held each June in the county seat, the Emmett Cherry Festival is Idaho's oldest and longest-running local event of its kind. Each year thousands turn out for the family-oriented event to celebrate the local harvest of cherries. Rising 5,906 feet, Squaw Butte stands at the north end of Gem County. Native Americans who used this area as their winter camp named the butte. Fur trappers roamed Gem County as early as 1818, but it wasn't until the 1860s that permanent settlements began in the area after gold was discovered in the nearby Boise Basin.

Next stop: A short, 110-mile flight southeast over Ada and Elmore counties to Gooding County.

Brainstorm

This county seat of Gem County hosts an annual cherry festival that is the oldest event of its kind in Idaho.

Cities and towns: Bliss, Gooding, Hagerman and Wendell

- **Established**: 1913
- **Named for**: Frank Gooding, seventh governor of Idaho (1905-09) and U.S. senator (1921-28)
- **County seat**: Gooding
- **Area**: 731 square miles
- **Elevation**: 3,573 feet
- **Latitude and longitude**: 42.93 degrees north; 114.71 degrees west

The scenic Thousand Springs make tourism an important industry in Gooding County and the rest of the Magic Valley. An abundance of natural springs gush from the steep canyon walls and cascade into the Snake River below. The water source is the Snake River Plain Aquifer, one of the largest groundwater systems in the world. The Niagara Springs National Natural Landmark is part of the system. Other landmarks in Gooding County are the Gooding City of Rocks, the Box Canyon Springs Natural Preserve and the Malad Gorge. The Malad Gorge is a narrow canyon formed by the Malad River. Dairy farming is also one of Gooding County's main industries. The county is one of the largest trout-producing areas in the United States. The county seat of the same name is the home of the Idaho School for the Deaf and the Blind. Mountain men and fur traders trapped and hunted along the Malad River extensively in the early 1800s. Settlers came to the rich agricultural lands of the Hagerman Valley in the 1860s. **Next stop**: Ida takes off and heads 218 miles north, rising over the Sawtooth, Boise and Payette national forests to Idaho County.

Brainstorm

This narrow canyon in Gooding County is one of the Magic Valley's most scenic landmarks.

IDAHO COUNTY

GRANGEVILLE

Cities and towns: Burgdorf, Clearwater, Cottonwood, Dixie, Elk City, Fenn, Ferdinand, Golden, Grangeville, Greencreek, Kooskia, Lowell, Lucile, Mount Idaho, Orogrande, Pollock, Red River Hot Springs, Riggins, Stites, Syringa, Warren and White Bird

- **Established**: 1864
- **Named for**: Columbia River steamship "Idaho," launched in 1860
- **County seat**: Grangeville
- **Area**: 8,485 square miles
- **Elevation**: 3,323 feet
- **Latitude and longitude**: 45.92 degrees north; 116.12 degrees west

Idaho County is the largest county in size in the Gem State. How big is it? Excluding the counties of Alaska, it is the 18th largest county in the United States. It's larger than six states. Idaho County is so big that it covers two time zones. Most of the county is in the Pacific time zone, but the town of Riggins and the rest of the area south of the Salmon River are in the Mountain time zone. The county seat of Grangeville was established during the north Idaho gold rush of the 1860s. Miners who followed the Nez Perce Trail into the Elk City Basin established the first settlements in the area.

The county is named for the Columbia River steamship "Idaho" that was launched in 1860 and transported miners during the gold rush. The Camas Prairie, Nez Perce National Forest and Clearwater Mountains cover much of Idaho County. The Salmon, Clearwater and Snake rivers provide miles of trout fishing opportunities, and the hundreds of miles of forests and mountains are a big draw for hunters. **Next stop**: A 258-mile flight southeast over the Gospel-Hump and the Lost River Range, descending over Mud Lake and landing in Jefferson County.

Brainstorm

A mountain range and a river in Idaho County share this name.

Cities and towns: Hamer, Lewisville, Menan, Monteview, Mud Lake, Rigby, Ririe, Roberts and Terreton

eastern 1J jefferson

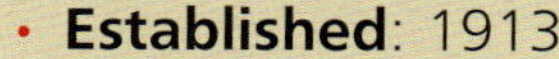

- **Established**: 1913
- **Named for**: Thomas Jefferson, third president of the United States
- **County seat**: Rigby
- **Area**: 1,095 square miles
- **Elevation**: 4,850 feet
- **Latitude and longitude**: 43.67 degrees north; 111.91 degrees west

The North Menan Butte National Natural Landmark is in Jefferson County and extends into Madison County. The area features two extinct volcanoes that were created by violent eruptions 10,000 years ago. They were formed when their lava met the cold water of the Snake River, creating an unusual cone formation that is found in only a few places in the world. The Camas National Wildlife Refuge is also in Jefferson County. The 10,578-acre refuge provides wildlife habitat and nesting grounds for migratory birds and waterfowl. Inventor Philo Farnsworth grew up in Jefferson County in the early 20th century. He is best known for inventing the first electronic television system. Farnsworth visualized the TV when he was a student at Rigby High School and later transmitted his first television picture in 1927. He is called "the father of television," but he received more than 150 patents for many other inventions. They include devices that led to the making of radar and the electron microscope. Two other famous residents of Jefferson County are author Vardis Fisher and Larry Wilson, a member of the Pro Football Hall of Fame with the St. Louis Cardinals. **Next stop**: Ida takes a 146-mile trip west across the Snake River Plain to Jerome County.

Brainstorm

This national wildlife refuge in Jefferson County provides wildlife habitat for many species of birds.

JEROME COUNTY

Ruins at Minidoka National Historic Site

Cities and towns: Eden, Hazelton and Jerome

- **Established**: 1919
- **Named for**: Irrigation project director Jerome Hill, his son-in-law Jerome Kuhn and grandson Jerome Kuhn Jr.
- **County seat**: Jerome
- **Area**: 600 square miles
- **Elevation**: 3,763 feet
- **Latitude and longitude**: 42.72 degrees north; 114.51 degrees west

Located in the middle of southern Idaho's Magic Valley, Jerome County is the fourth-smallest of Idaho's 44 counties in terms of size. The Minidoka Relocation Center was located near the town of Eden in Jerome County. The center was one of 10 Japanese-American internment camps set up by the United States government during World War II. More than 9,000 Japanese-American citizens and resident aliens from Idaho, Oregon, Washington and Alaska were detained at the camp from 1942-45. The camp is now a U.S. national historic site. Visitors can see the remains of the entry guard station and waiting room as well as the camp's rock garden. A Japanese-American relocation camp exhibit is also on display at the Jerome County Museum in the county seat of Jerome. The city of Jerome is also the home of the Idaho Farm and Ranch Agricultural Museum. The museum has displays of old farm equipment and original buildings from the surrounding area. Agriculture is the primary industry in Jerome County. **Next stop**: A 362-mile trip northwest over the Boise and Payette national forests and the Salmon River Mountains to Kootenai County.

Brainstorm

Given the fertile soil in the Magic Valley, it is no surprise that this is Jerome County's main industry.

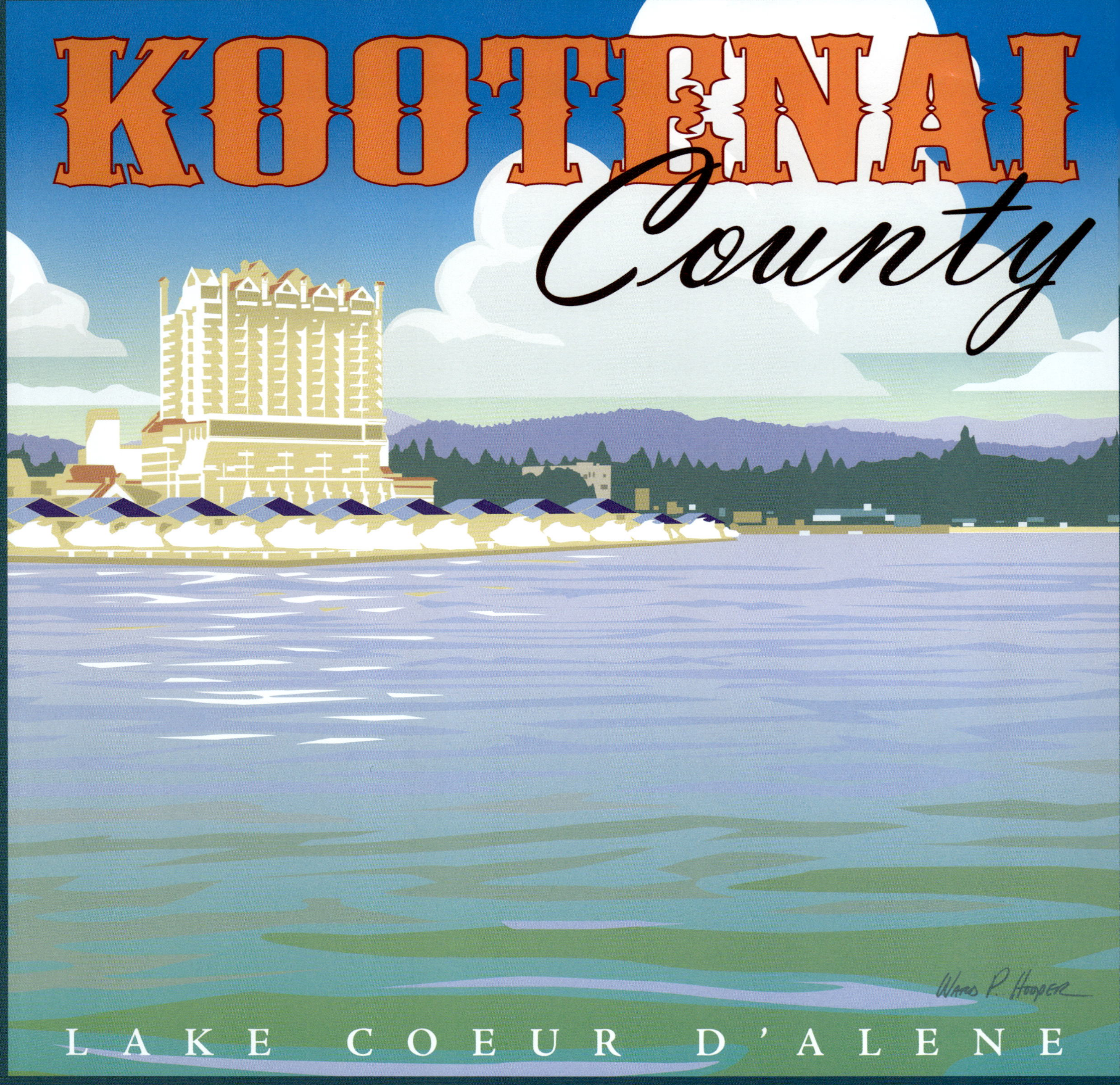

Cities and towns: Athol, Cataldo, Coeur d'Alene, Dalton Gardens, Fernan Lake Village, Garwood, Harrison, Hauser, Hayden, Hayden Lake, Huetter, Post Falls, Rathdrum, Spirit Lake, State Line and Worley

- **Established**: 1864
- **Named for**: Native American tribe
- **County seat**: Coeur d'Alene
- **Area**: 1,245 square miles
- **Elevation**: 2,157 feet
- **Latitude and longitude:** 47.69 degrees north; 116.78 degrees west

Scenic and popular Kootenai County is one of Idaho's largest counties in population. It is surrounded by mountains and contains more than 20 lakes, including Lake Coeur d'Alene. The lake shares its name with the county seat. It is 25 miles long, ranges from 1 to 3 miles wide, and has more than 100 miles of shoreline for boaters and vacationers to enjoy. Coeur d'Alene Parkway is a popular roadway that follows the north shore of Lake Coeur d'Alene. Tourism is one of Kootenai County's main industries. The Mission of the Sacred Heart near the town of Cataldo is the oldest standing building in Idaho and a national historic landmark. Catholic missionaries arrived at the invitation of the Coeur d'Alene Native American tribe in the early 1840s and built the church in the early 1850s. Farragut State Park is in northern Kootenai County. Located on the southern part of Lake Pend Oreille, the 4,000-acre park was formerly the Farragut Naval Training Station during World War II. At the time it was the world's second-largest naval training base. Kootenai County is the home of North Idaho College. **Next stop**: Ida flies 67 miles south to Latah County.

Brainstorm

This state park on Lake Pend Oreille in Kootenai County was a naval training station during World War II.

Cities and towns: Bovill, Deary, Genesee, Juliaetta, Kendrick, Moscow, Onaway, Potlatch and Troy

- **Established**: 1888
- **Named for**: Latah Creek
- **County seat**: Moscow
- **Area**: 1,077 square miles
- **Elevation**: 2,579 feet
- **Latitude and longitude**: 46.72 degrees north; 116.99 degrees west

Latah County is part of a region in northern Idaho and eastern Washington called the Palouse. The area is famous for its rolling hills and rich agriculture. The Palouse is known for its production of lentils, peas, wheat and barley. But Latah County also has thick forests of pine, fir and cedar. Before homesteaders arrived, the Nez Perce and Palouse Native American tribes who wintered along the Clearwater and Snake rivers traveled to Latah County in the spring and summer to dig camas roots, fish, hunt and pick huckleberries. Latah County is the only county in the U.S. established by an act of Congress. During the 1860s, Latah County was a base camp for the gold rush in northern Idaho. The county seat of Moscow is the home of the University of Idaho. The U of I was established in 1889, the year before Idaho became a state. The McConnell Mansion in Moscow was built in the late 1800s by Gov. William McConnell. The building is now used by the Latah County Historical Society for displays of period furniture and relics. **Next stop**: A 182-mile flight heading southeast over the Clearwater and Salmon River mountains to Lemhi County.

Brainstorm

Latah County is part of this region that is famous for its rolling hills and rich farmland.

Cities and towns: Leadore, Lemhi, North Fork, Salmon, Shoup and Tendoy

- **Established**: 1869
- **Named for**: Limhi, figure in the Book of Mormon
- **County seat**: Salmon
- **Area**: 4,564 square miles
- **Elevation**: 4,040 feet
- **Latitude and longitude**: 45.17 degrees north; 113.89 degrees west

Lemhi County is one of Idaho's most historic counties because of Lewis and Clark, the explorers who passed through the area in 1805. Lewis and Clark named the Salmon River the "River of No Return" during their historic exploration of the western United States. The Lemhi Pass National Historic Landmark near the town of Tendoy is the point where Lewis and Clark crossed the Continental Divide on their expedition. Sacajawea, the Shoshone woman famous for her role in the Lewis and Clark Expedition, was born in the Lemhi River Valley in 1788. Today Lemhi County is filled with thousands of miles of back country roads and trails. The Salmon River provides whitewater rafting and some of the best steelhead and salmon fishing in the western United States. Lemhi County also has some of the best big game hunting in the West. The county's rural terrain is also ideal for hiking, backpacking, horseback riding, camping, snowmobiling and cross-country skiing. In addition, Idaho's third-largest county borders the 2.3 million-acre Frank Church River of No Return Wilderness Area. Tourism and ranching are among the biggest industries in Lemhi County. **Next stop**: A 173-mile trip northwest through Idaho County to Lewis County.

Brainstorm

This river in Lemhi County is also called the River of No Return.

Cities and towns: Craigmont, Kamiah, Nezperce, Reubens and Winchester

- **Established**: 1911
- **Named for**: Meriwether Lewis, leader of the Lewis and Clark Expedition
- **County seat**: Nezperce
- **Area**: 479 square miles
- **Elevation**: 3,215 feet
- **Latitude and longitude**: 46.23 degrees north; 116.23 degrees west

Lewis County is one of Idaho's smallest counties in both size and population. The county is a large part of north central Idaho's Camas Prairie (not to be confused with the Camas Prairie in south central Idaho), a major grain-producing region. The Clearwater River flows through the north part of the county while the Salmon River flows through the south end. Both river areas are filled with Douglas fir and ponderosa pine. Lewis County is named for Meriwether Lewis of the Lewis and Clark Expedition. The expedition spent a month in the Clearwater River Valley near what is now the town of Kamiah on its return from the Pacific coast in May 1806. The Nez Perce Indians made this area their home and knew no pioneers until the Lewis and Clark Expedition. There are 22 miles of Lewis and Clark Trail in Lewis County. Winchester Lake State Park surrounds a 103-acre lake in a forested area at the foot of the Craig Mountains. Located on the banks of the Clearwater River, the Heart of the Monster monument is a rock formation that commemorates the legendary birthplace of the Nez Perce tribe. **Next stop**: A 244-mile trip heading southeast over the Clearwater, Salmon River and Sawtooth mountains to Lincoln County.

Brainstorm

The county seat of Lewis County is named for this Native American tribe.

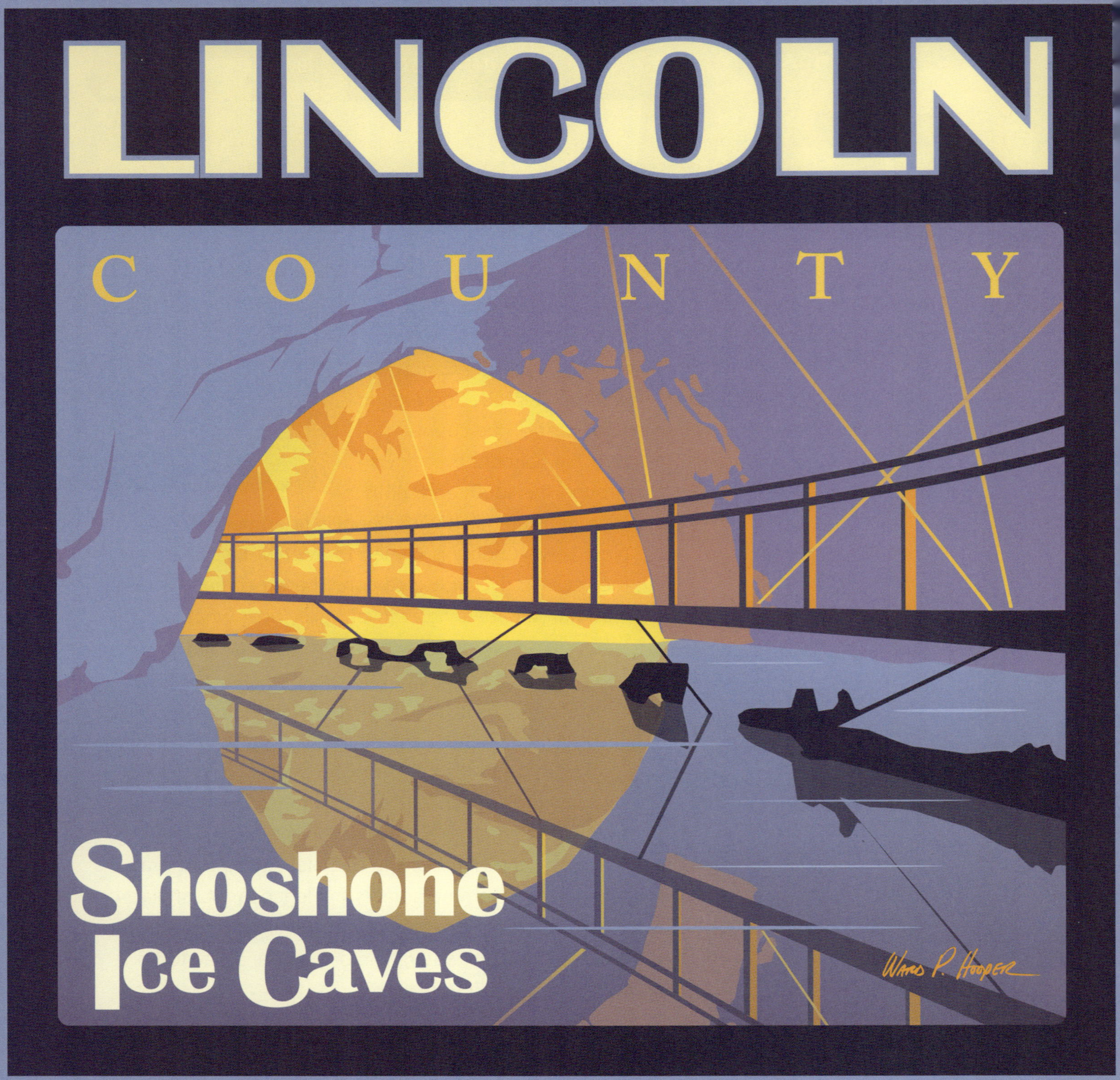

LINCOLN

C O U N T Y

Shoshone Ice Caves

Ward P. Hooper

Cities and towns: Dietrich, Richfield and Shoshone

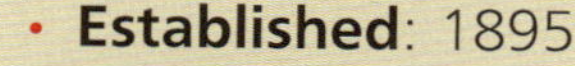

- **Established**: 1895
- **Named for**: Abraham Lincoln, 16th president of the United States, who was in office when Idaho territory was founded
- **County seat**: Shoshone
- **Area**: 1,206 square miles
- **Elevation**: 3,967 feet
- **Latitude and longitude**: 42.93 degrees north; 114.40 degrees west

White settlers moved into Lincoln County in the early 1880s. The early homesteaders used the area for farming and raising sheep. Basque shepherds still herd sheep in Lincoln County. Farming and ranching are the area's main industries. The main crops grown in Lincoln County are potatoes, beans, wheat, barley, corn, sugar beets and onions. The county was much larger when it was established in 1895. When Gooding and Minidoka counties were established 18 years later, the change took about half of the original Lincoln County land.

After Jerome County was established in 1919, Lincoln County was left with only 1,206 square miles. One of Lincoln County's main landforms is the Shoshone Ice Caves—large lava caves that stay cold with an ice floor year-round. The caves feature a lava tunnel that is 1,000 feet long and varies between 8 and 30 feet in height. A nearby museum contains Indian artifacts, gems and minerals. Lincoln County is one of 17 counties in the United States named after Abraham Lincoln. **Next stop**: A 144-mile flight northeast over the Craters of the Moon National Monument and Preserve and the Big Southern Butte to Madison County.

Brainstorm

A Native American tribe, the county seat, and the popular ice caves in Lincoln County share this name.

Cities and towns: Rexburg and Sugar City

- **Established**: 1913
- **Named for**: James Madison, fourth president of the United States
- **County seat**: Rexburg
- **Area**: 472 square miles
- **Elevation**: 4,861 feet
- **Latitude and longitude**: 43.82 degrees north; 111.78 degrees west

Madison County's first settlers were Mormon pioneers from Utah who built farms and roads. They installed the area's first irrigation system, using the waters of the Snake River. The majority of Madison County's residents are members of the Mormon church. The county seat of Rexburg was severely damaged by the Teton Dam flood in June 1976. The Teton River flows through northern Rexburg, and the flood left most of the city underwater for several days after the dam collapsed. The basement of the Rexburg Tabernacle houses the Teton Dam Flood Museum. The tabernacle was built in 1911 and was registered as a national historic site in 1974. The 1,000-seat building is used as a civic auditorium and is well known for its excellent acoustics and pipe organ. Madison County is the home of Brigham Young University-Idaho. The university began as a high school-level academy in 1888 and was eventually established as Ricks College, a two-year school named in honor of Mormon pioneer and city founder, Thomas Ricks. In 2001 Ricks became a four-year college and assumed the name BYU-Idaho. **Next stop**: Ida takes off and heads back to the Magic Valley, 126 miles southwest to Minidoka County.

Brainstorm

This Mormon pioneer was the founder of Rexburg, the county seat of Madison County.

Cities and towns: Heyburn, Minidoka, Paul and Rupert

- **Established**: 1913
- **Named for**: Native American sayings for "a fountain of water" or "a broad expanse"
- **County seat**: Rupert
- **Area**: 760 square miles
- **Elevation**: 4,206 feet
- **Latitude and longitude**: 42.61 degrees north; 113.67 degrees west

Minidoka County's history is closely tied to the Bureau of Reclamation. The bureau is the section of the U.S. Department of the Interior that oversees water resource management in the western United States. In 1902 President Theodore Roosevelt signed the Reclamation Act and created the Minidoka Project. The project led to the construction of the Minidoka Dam, the first Bureau of Reclamation project in Idaho. The dam was finished in 1906. By 1909 the dam's power plant was completed. It was the first federal power plant in the Northwest. The Minidoka Dam was the first of five dams built in the Minidoka Project, which was designed to bring water to the farming areas near the county seat of Rupert and other towns. Lake Walcott was created by the Minidoka Dam. The 11,000-acre lake is a popular area for camping and fishing. The near-by Minidoka National Wildlife Refuge attracts up to 100,000 ducks and geese during their spring and fall migrations. Built around 1920, the Wilson Theatre in Rupert is on the National Register of Historic Places. **Next stop**: Ida heads 309 north-west, flying over the Sawtooth, Boise and Payette national forests to Nez Perce County.

Brainstorm

This 11,000-acre lake in Minidoka County was created when the Minidoka Dam was built.

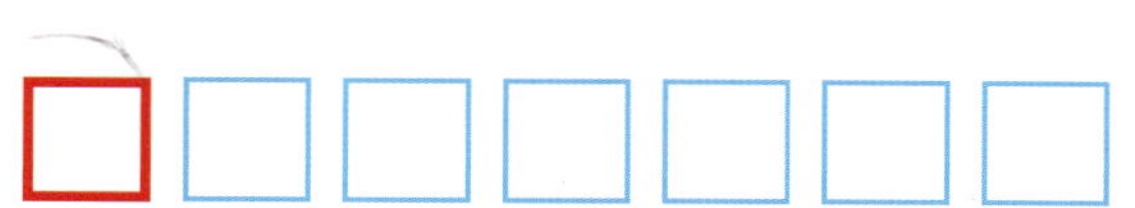

Cities and towns: Culdesac, Gifford, Lapwai, Leland, Lenore, Lewiston, Myrtle, Peck, Southwick, Spalding and Waha

- **Established**: 1864
- **Named for**: Native American tribe
- **County seat**: Lewiston
- **Area**: 849 square miles
- **Elevation**: 738 feet
- **Latitude and longitude**: 46.39 degrees north; 116.99 degrees west

For thousands of years the area that is now Nez Perce County was the home of the Native American tribe of the same name. The Nez Perce National Historical Park commemorates the Nez Perce people and their life with the white explorers, fur traders, missionaries, settlers and gold miners who moved through or into the area. The first pioneers the Nez Perce met were the members of the Lewis and Clark Expedition in 1805. The northern portion of the county is part of the Palouse, the wide and rolling agricultural region of the Middle Columbia Basin. Nez Perce County is the home of Lewis-Clark State College. The county seat of Lewiston is unusual in that it is an inland seaport and the lowest point in Idaho at 710 feet above sea level. Ships come from the Pacific Ocean and travel inland more than 450 miles on the Columbia and Snake rivers to reach Lewiston. Hells Gate State Park is the gateway to Lewis and Clark country and Hells Canyon, the deepest river gorge in North America. **Next stop**: A 373-mile flight, heading south-east through the middle of the state to Oneida County.

Brainstorm

This county seat of Nez Perce County has the lowest elevation in Idaho at 710 feet above sea level.

Oneida County

RESERVOIRS, LAKES & STREAMS

Cities and towns: Holbrook, Malad City, Pleasantview, Samaria and Stone

- **Established**: 1864
- **Named for**: Oneida Lake in New York, the home state of many of its settlers
- **County seat**: Malad City
- **Area**: 1,200 square miles
- **Elevation**: 4,551 feet
- **Latitude and longitude**: 42.18 degrees north; 112.24 degrees west

With a wealth of reservoirs, lakes and streams Oneida County offers outstanding fishing, swimming and boating opportunities. The Malad River (not to be confused with the Gooding County river with the same name) as well as nine reservoirs make fishing a year-round attraction in the area. Daniels Reservoir is famous for its prize-winning trout, and kokanee salmon can also be found in several of the reservoirs. The area also has miles of trails accessible by foot, horseback and all-terrain vehicles. The northern part of the county is on the fringe of the Caribou-Targhee and Sawtooth national forests. In the 1860s the county seat was moved from Soda Springs to Malad City because of Malad's location on the stagecoach line and freight route between northern Utah and the mines of Butte, Montana. Established in 1864, Malad is one of the oldest communities in Idaho.

The Oneida County Courthouse in Malad City is listed on the National Register of Historic Places. The Oneida County Pioneer Museum in Malad City and the 47,000-acre Curlew National Grassland are two of the county's main attractions. The grassland provides habitat for waterfowl, songbirds, birds of prey and upland game birds. **Next stop**: A 232-mile flight west along Idaho's southern border to Owyhee County.

Brainstorm

This body of water in Oneida County is famous for the excellent fishing it offers.

OWYHEE

COUNTY

THE CANYONLANDS

Cities and towns: Bruneau, Grand View, Homedale, Marsing and Murphy

- **Established**: 1863
- **Named for**: Taken from a pronunciation of "Hawaii," after Hawaiian fur trappers who explored the area in the early 1820s
- **County seat**: Murphy
- **Area**: 7,678 square miles
- **Elevation**: 2,802 feet
- **Latitude and longitude**: 43.21 degrees north; 116.55 degrees west

Idaho's second-largest county in size, Owhyee County features the Bruneau Dunes and the Bruneau River Canyon, among other natural attractions. In Bruneau Dunes State Park, the tallest single-structured sand dune in North America rises to 470 feet above the nearby lakes and marshes on the Owhyee County desert. The Bruneau Canyon Overlook provides a spectacular view of the desert gorge of the Bruneau River. The canyon is 1,300 feet wide, has an 800-foot drop, and is 60 miles long. Owyhee County's history is linked to Idaho's mining boom in the 1880s. The county is named for the river, mountains and mining area explored by Hawaiian fur trappers in the early 1820s. Hawaii and Owyhee are different spellings of the same word. Gold was discovered on Jordan Creek in 1863, and millions of dollars of gold and silver were taken from the area until the industry declined in the early 1900s. Silver City and Ruby City remain ghost towns from that period. At its height in the 1880s, Owyhee County was among the most densely populated places in Idaho. Today it has one of the state's smallest populations. **Next stop**: An 81-mile flight north to Payette County.

Brainstorm

Located in Owyhee County, these are the tallest single-structure sand dunes in North America.

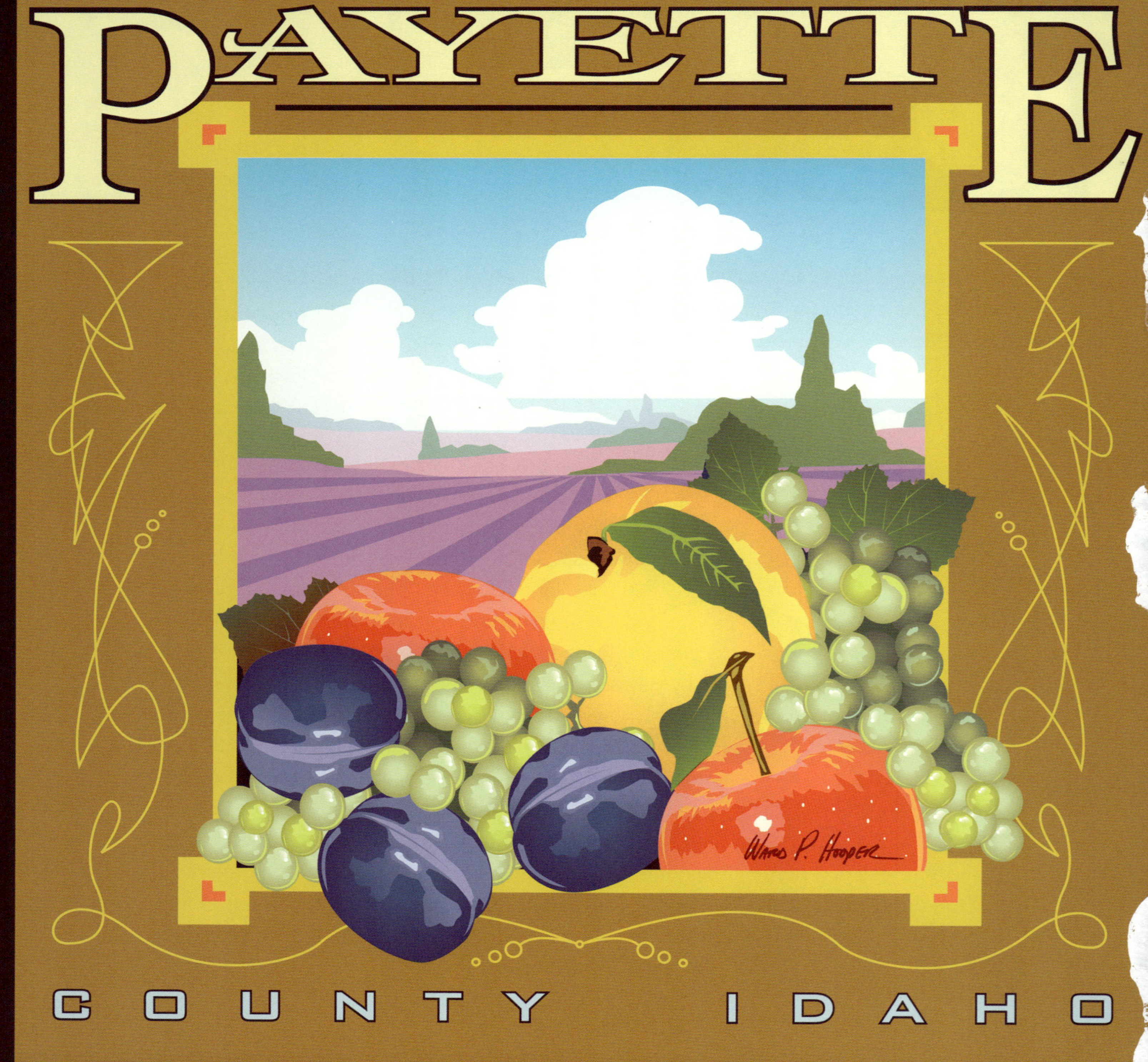

Cities and towns: Fruitland, New Plymouth and Payette

- **Established**: 1917
- **Named for**: Francois Payette, Canadian-born fur trader and early settler
- **County seat**: Payette
- **Area**: 408 square miles
- **Elevation**: 2,150 feet
- **Latitude and longitude**: 44.07 degrees north; 116.92 degrees west

Idaho's smallest county in size, Payette County is on the Oregon-Idaho border where the Snake and Payette rivers meet. During the westward migration of thousands of immigrants in the late 19th century, Payette County saw miners, explorers and pioneers travel through the area. Homesteaders who remained in what is now Payette County built irrigation systems. The community grew rapidly, and the fertile valley became famous for its large harvests of fruit and vegetables. A base camp for the Oregon Short Line Railroad was constructed in Payette County in the mid-1800s. The river was named after Francois Payette, an early settler in the area. The camp, named Boomerang, was renamed Payette after the Payette River and became the county seat. By the turn of the century, there was more produce grown and shipped from the Payette County area than any other state in the nation. Payette hosts the Apple Blossom Festival each May. Today, the Payette River is a popular spot for boating, fishing and tubing. Payette County is the home of major league baseball star Harmon Killebrew, who was inducted into baseball's Hall of Fame in 1984 as a member of the Minnesota Twins. **Next stop**: Ida hops on her plane and heads 223 miles east to Power County.

Brainstorm

This winding Idaho river flows into the Payette River in Payette County.

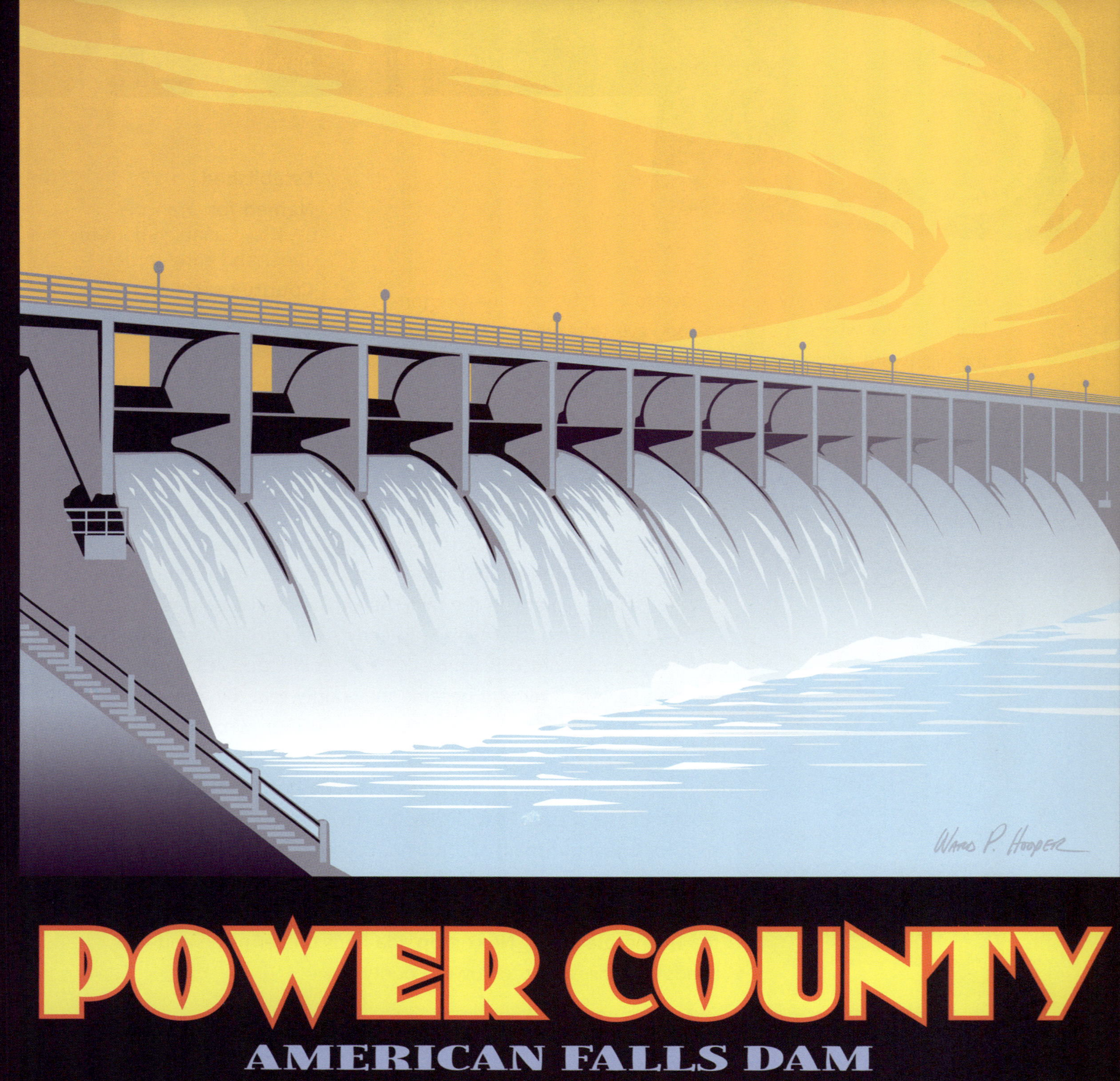

Cities and towns: American Falls, Arbon Valley, and Rockland

- **Established**: 1913
- **Named for**: American Falls power plant
- **County seat**: American Falls
- **Area**: 1,406 square miles
- **Elevation**: 4,330 feet
- **Latitude and longitude**: 42.78 degrees north; 112.85 degrees west

American Falls, Power County's largest city and county seat, was a campsite on the old Oregon Trail along the Snake River. Power County is famous for its extensive irrigation projects. The American Falls Dam and the reservoir it forms are a part of the Minidoka Irrigation Project on the Snake River Plain and are used primarily for flood control, irrigation and recreation. When the original dam was built by the Bureau of Reclamation in 1927, the residents of American Falls were forced to relocate three-quarters of their town to make room for the reservoir. In 1978 the original dam was demolished after a second dam, also called the American Falls Dam, was completed.

Shoshone and Bannock Native American tribes have lived in Power County for more than 10,000 years.

Agriculture is the county's main industry, particularly the growing of sugar beets and potatoes. The Snake River and the American Falls Reservoir offer many opportunities for boating and fishing. Massacre Rocks State Park provides camping, river access, hiking and fishing. **Next stop**: A 356-mile flight north over the Salmon-Challis, Nez Perce and Clearwater national forests, veering west of the Bitterroot National Forest to Shoshone County.

Brainstorm

This Native American tribe has lived in Power County for thousands of years.

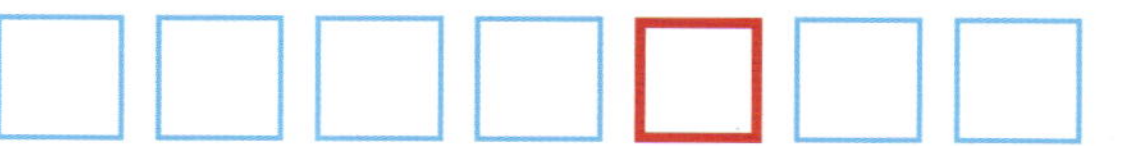

Cities and towns: Kellogg, Mullan, Osburn, Pinehurst, Smelterville, Wallace and Wardner

northern S shoshone

- **Established**: 1864
- **Named for**: Native American tribe
- **County seat**: Wallace
- **Area**: 2,634 square miles
- **Elevation**: 2,730 feet
- **Latitude and longitude**: 47.47 degrees north; 115.92 degrees west

Commonly called the Silver Valley because of its mining history, Shoshone County is famous for the vast amounts of silver, lead and zinc taken from its mines. Several of the world's largest and deepest silver mines are found near Wallace, the county seat. In 1890 Shoshone County was the most populated county in the new state of Idaho, and Wallace was the third-largest city in the state with 2,000 residents. Unfortunately, Shoshone County's history includes periods of conflict and hostilities between miners and mine owners. In 1892 several miners were killed during a shooting as they protested wage cuts. Violence erupted again in 1899 when some miners dynamited a mill after 17 miners were fired for joining a union. About one-third of Wallace was destroyed by the Great Fire of 1910, the largest forest fire in U.S. history that burned 3 million acres in Washington, Idaho and Montana. In May of 1972 a fire broke out deep in the Sunshine Mine near the city of Kellogg. Eighty-three miners were rescued, but 91 men died in the worst mining disaster in the nation in more than 50 years. A memorial statue outside of Kellogg honors those who died in the disaster. **Next stop**: Ida heads 347 miles southeast to Teton County.

Brainstorm

Along with silver and zinc, this is one of the main minerals mined in Shoshone County.

Cities and towns: Driggs, Tetonia and Victor

- **Established**: 1915
- **Named for**: Teton mountain range and valley
- **County seat**: Driggs
- **Area**: 450 square miles
- **Elevation**: 6,109 feet
- **Latitude and longitude:** 43.72 degrees north; 111.10 degrees west

Teton County may be the second-smallest county in size in the Gem State, but it is also the highest with its county seat of Driggs sitting at an elevation of more than 6,000 feet above sea level. The Teton Valley was formerly known as Pierre's Hole where Native American tribes held their councils and trappers met to trade furs and other goods. Located on the Wyoming border, Teton County is east of the majestic Teton Mountain Range. Some of the best skiing and snowboarding in North America is available near Teton County, including Grand Targhee Resort, located 12 miles east of Driggs in Alta, Wyoming. Tourism is a growing industry in Teton County. In addition to skiing, local outfitters and guides in and around Teton County offer everything from fishing and hunting to mountain biking and hot air balloon or glider rides over the valley. Driggs also hosts cultural events that include the Teton Valley Summer Festival in July and Music on Main each Thursday in July and August. **Next stop**: A 188-mile flight southwest over the Caribou-Targhee National Forest, across the eastern portion of the Snake River Plain, and into the center of the Magic Valley and Twin Falls County.

Brainstorm

This town in Teton County is more than 6,000 feet above sea level and the highest county seat in Idaho.

TWIN FALLS COUNTY

PERRINE BRIDGE

Ward P. Hooper

Cities and towns: Buhl, Castleford, Filer, Hansen, Hollister, Kimberly, Murtaugh and Twin Falls

- **Established**: 1907
- **Named for**: Twin Falls waterfall on the Snake River
- **County seat**: Twin Falls
- **Area**: 1,925 square miles
- **Elevation**: 3,745 feet
- **Latitude and longitude**: 42.56 degrees north; 114.46 degrees west

Twin Falls County is the home of some of Idaho's most spectacular landforms and man-made structures, including Shoshone Falls, the Hagerman Fossil Beds National Monument, Balanced Rock and the Perrine Bridge. At 212 feet, Shoshone Falls are higher than Niagara Falls. They are best viewed during the spring and early summer when water flows are high and not reduced by irrigation. The Hagerman Fossil Beds protect some of the world's richest fossil deposits from 3.5 million years ago. Balanced Rock is a cyclone-shaped basalt rock that rises 48 feet in the air above the Salmon Falls Creek Canyon northwest of Castleford. The Perrine Bridge is a four-lane bridge on U.S. Highway 93 over the Snake River Canyon north of the county seat of Twin Falls. The structure is approximately 1,500 feet long and 486 feet above the Snake River. The original bridge was the highest bridge in the world when it was built in 1927. The current bridge was completed in 1976, and the original bridge was demolished. Twin Falls County is the home of the College of Southern Idaho, a two-year school in the city of Twin Falls. **Next stop**: A 157-mile trip northwest to Valley County.

Brainstorm

Some of the world's richest fossil deposits are found in these fossil beds in Twin Falls County.

VALLEY

COUNTY

PAYETTE LAKE, MCCALL

Cities and towns: Cascade, Donnelly and McCall

- **Established**: 1917
- **Named for**: Long Valley
- **County seat**: Cascade
- **Area**: 3,678 square miles
- **Elevation**: 4,760 feet
- **Latitude and longitude**: 44.51 degrees north; 116.04 degrees west

Numerous outdoor sports and recreation opportunities and the resort city of McCall make tourism one of the leading industries in Valley County. McCall is on the southern shore of Payette Lake near the center of the Payette National Forest. Originally a logging town, McCall is now an all-season tourist destination. The area's rivers, streams and mountain lakes offer a variety of warm-weather water sports that include fishing, boating, swimming and rafting. In the winter Valley County offers hundreds of miles of snow-mobile and cross-county skiing trails as well as downhill skiing. Valley County is known for its annual McCall Winter Carnival, extended winters, and the highest average snowfall in the state. Shoshone and Nez Perce tribes were among the first inhabitants of what is now Valley County. Ponderosa State Park was established in 1965 on a 1,000-acre peninsula 2 miles outside of McCall. The park is home to some of the largest old-growth trees in the western United States. Valley County gets its name from Long Valley of the North Fork of the Payette River, which extends more than 30 miles from Payette Lake at McCall south to Cascade to Round Valley. **Next stop**: Ida's final trip is also her shortest—just a 49-mile flight to neighboring Washington County.

Brainstorm

The resort town of McCall in Valley County is on the shore of this scenic lake.

Cities and towns: Cambridge, Midvale and Weiser

- **Established**: 1879
- **Named for**: George Washington, first president of the United States
- **County seat**: Weiser
- **Area**: 1,456 square miles
- **Elevation**: 2,130 feet
- **Latitude and longitude**: 44.25 degrees north; 116.96 degrees west

Every June since 1953, Washington County's largest city and county seat of Weiser has attracted world-class musicians for the National Ole Time Fiddlers' Contest and Festival. The annual festival draws national media coverage and more than 7,000 people to the area. More than 300 fiddle-playing contestants compete in eight divisions in the weeklong event. Fiddle music first came to Washington County around 1863. The music was played by the covered wagon pioneers who stopped in the area. Washington County is located where the Weiser and Snake rivers meet near the Idaho-Oregon border. Weiser is named for Peter Weiser, an American soldier and member of the Lewis and Clark Expedition. Built in 1904, the Pythian Castle in Weiser is an excellent example of early architecture in Idaho. The sandstone for the building was hauled by wagon to the town, where it was hand cut. Other historic buildings in Washington County include the Galloway House and the Union Pacific Train Depot. Legendary pitcher Walter Johnson played semipro baseball for the Weiser Senators as a teenager in 1906-1907. Nicknamed the "Big Train," he once pitched 84 consecutive scoreless innings while in Weiser before starting his major league career with the Washington Senators. He was inducted into baseball's Hall of Fame in 1936.

Brainstorm

This musical instrument has a long history with Washington County and is the source of an annual gathering of world-class musicians.

Idaho License Plates

The 44 counties have been identified on Idaho's license plates since 1945. On the lines provided below, mark the 44 counties with their appropriate license plate prefix.

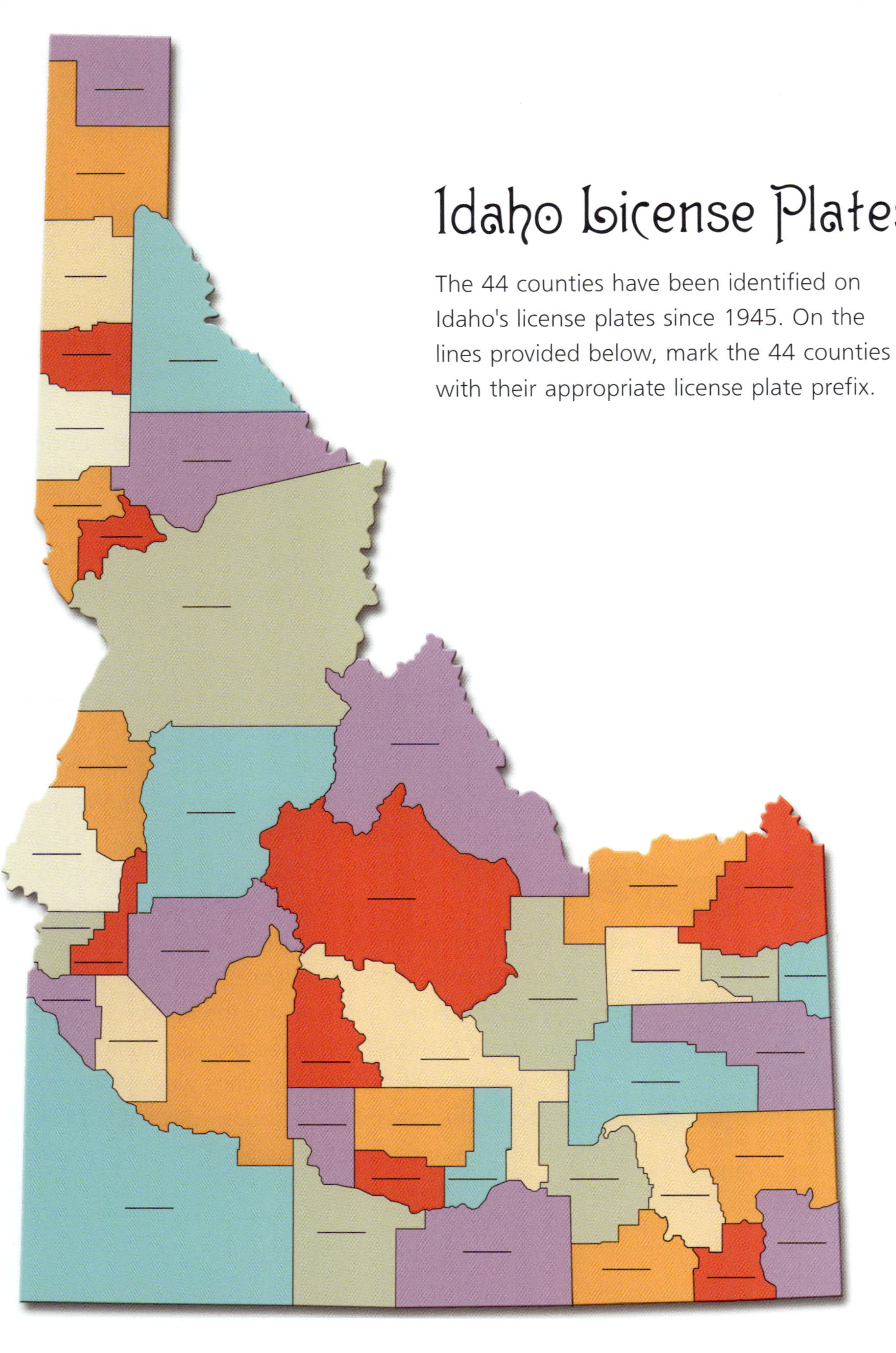

Complete the Puzzle

Each county brainstorm answer has a special letter in a red box. Use those 44 letters to spell out the first verse of "Here We Have Idaho", the state's official song.

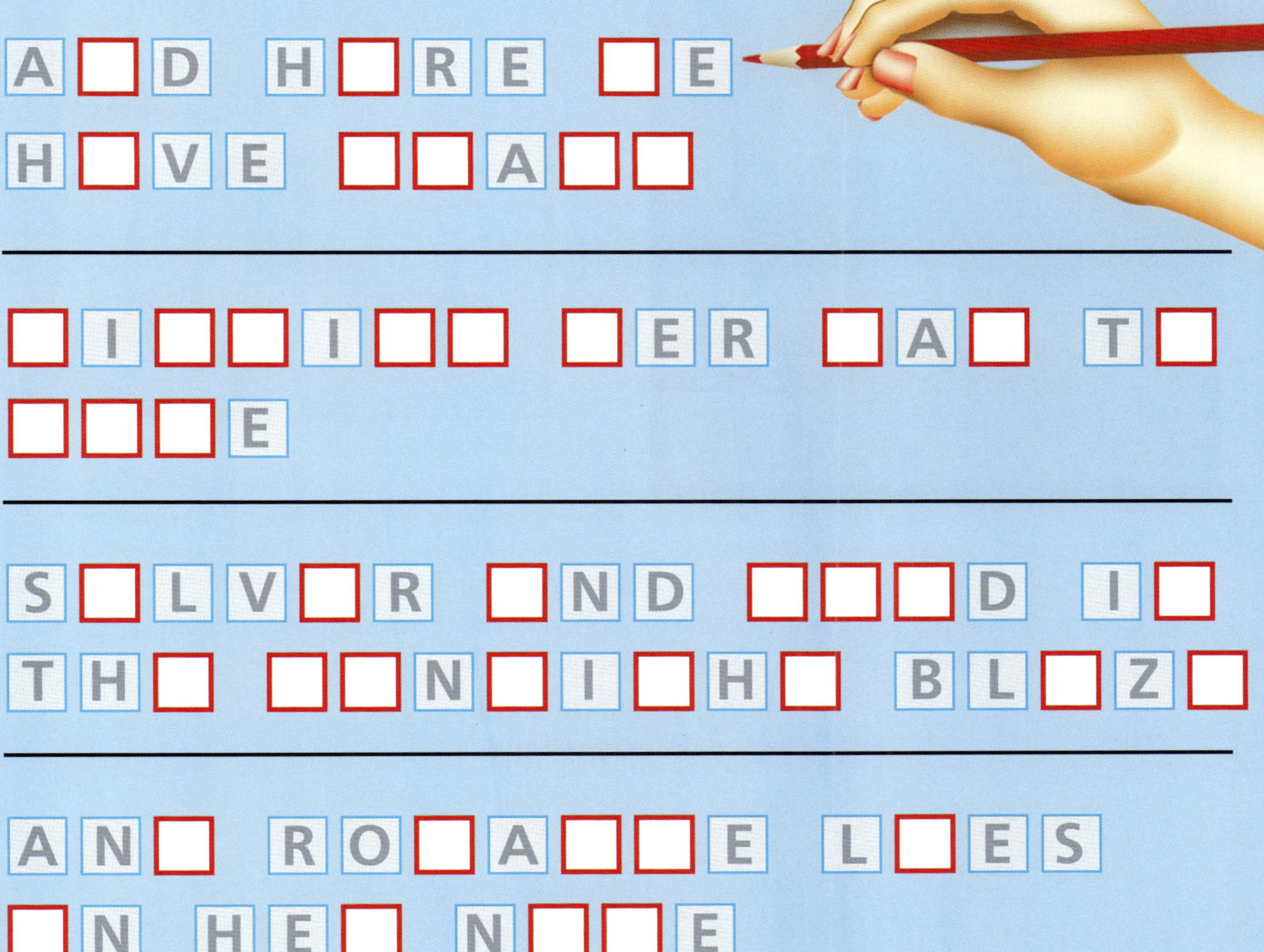

The answer to the puzzle is the first verse of the chorus to "Here We Have Idaho," our state song. Here is the completed verse:
And here we have Idaho; Winning her way to fame; Silver and gold in the sunlight blaze; And romance lies in her name.

How to Order

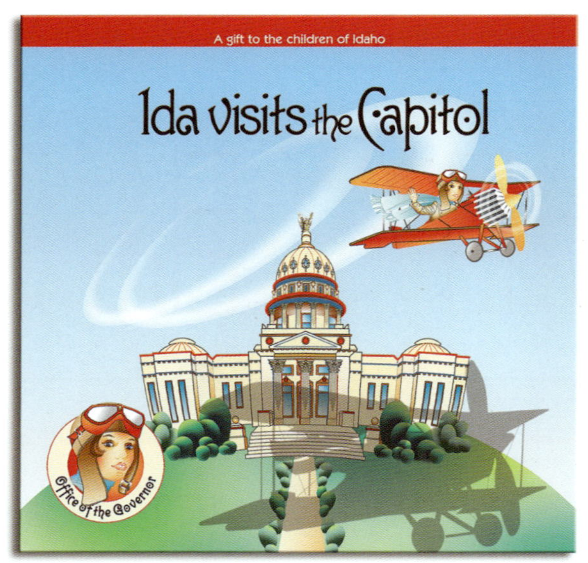

Ida Tours the 44 and *Ida Visits the Capitol* can be purchased from the Otter Education Series online catalog at **www.booksboisestate.com**. Or contact the Boise State University Publications Office at

books@boisestate.edu

(208) 426-1514.